CONSTRAINTS ON POLITICAL ORDER IN UGANDA

Jimmy Kazaara Tindigarukayo (PhD)

Senior Lecturer

Sir Arthur Lewis Institute of Social and Economic Studies,
University of the West Indies, Mona Campus, Kingston 7,
Jamaica, West Indies

CONSTRAINTS ON POLITICAL ORDER IN UGANDA

Jimmy Kazaara Tindigarukayo (PhD)

Kobalt Books

Saint Louis, MO

CONSTRAINTS ON POLITICAL ORDER IN UGANDA

For information:
Kobalt Books L.L.C.
P.O. Box 771912,
Saint Louis, MO 63177
Printed in the U.S.A

CHAPTER I
CONSTRAINTS ON POLITICAL ORDER IN UGANDA

INTRODUCTION

Political order, defined in terms of the absence of sustained societal conflict, violence, and instability has been an elusive goal rather than a reality in most developing countries, and more particularly those in Africa. Rather than moving towards political order thus defined, majority of African countries have been characterized by political instability, constitutional crises, breakdown of law and order, social and cultural conflict, military coups, economic dislocation, and the like. In other words, most African countries have been moving towards political disorder rather than order.

The main concerns of this study are three-fold: (i) to identify major constraints on political order in Uganda; (ii) to discuss the likely sources of those constraints and (iii) to provide some policy recommendations for their alleviation. I will now turn to a brief identification of individual constraints on political order in Uganda, from the colonial period up to the present.

- **Secessionist Attempts**: Secessionism, which entails the desire on the part of a sub-national group to break away from the existing political system, has been a common feature in Uganda. Between 1953 and 1966, Uganda experienced five secessionist attempts: three by the kingdom of Buganda in 1953, 1960, and 1966; and the other two by mountain ethnic groups--the Sebei of Mount Elgon and the Bamba and Bankonjo of Mount Rwenzori in 1961 and 1963, respectively.

- **Constitutional Crises:** Uganda has undergone nine major constitutional crises: (i) a long conflict between the kingdoms of Bunyoro and Buganda over the "lost counties", a territory of Bunyoro which was allocated to Buganda by the colonial power in return for the formers assistance in the imperial expansion in Uganda; (ii) a conflict between Governor Andrew Cohen and Kabaka (king) Edward Mutesa II of Buganda over the relationship between Buganda and the rest of Uganda, which resulted into the deportation of Mutesa to England and a declaration of state of emergency over Buganda in 1953; (iii) a conflict between Obote's central government and the local government of Buganda, arising mainly from the struggle for political control, which resulted into a limited civil war in Uganda in May 1966; (iv) a conflict between President Obote and his Military Commander, Idi Amin, which led to the military coup of January 1971; (v) a violent change of regime when Idi

Amin was forcefully removed from power in April 1979 by Tanzanian troops and Ugandan exiles; (vi) a conflict between President Yusuf Lule and the National Consultative Council (NCC) in June 1979, leading to the removal of the former from the presidency; (vii) a conflict between President Binaisa and the Military Commission in June 1980, which led to the latter's assumption of power; (viii) a conflict between President Obote and Acholi soldiers, leading to Obote's second removal from power through a military coup on 27 July 1985; and (ix) an armed conflict between Museveni's National Resistance Army (NRA) and Tito Okello's Uganda National Liberation Army (UNLA), arising mainly from a struggle for power, which ended in the latter's forceful removal from power by the former.

- **Civil Wars:** In addition to religious civil wars in Buganda at the turn of the century, Uganda has experienced six civil wars since independence: (i) an armed conflict between the local government of Buganda and troops of the central government of Uganda in May 1966; (ii) an armed conflict between Amin's troops and Ugandan exiles in September 1972; (iii) a war between Amin's army and Ugandan exiles, supported by Tanzanian troops, which resulted in the overthrow of Idi Amin from power in April 1979; (iv) a continuous armed conflict

9

(1980-1986) between Obote's second regime and three guerrilla movements in Uganda: Museveni's National Resistance Army (NRA), Kayiira's Uganda Freedom Army (UFA), and Moses Ali's Uganda National Rescue Front (UNRF),(v) a war between the Uganda army and Museveni's NRA guerrilla force, leading to the victory of the latter in January 1986, and (vi) the current armed conflict between Museveni's government and two rebel forces: the Lords' Resistance Army in the northern part of Uganda and the Allied Democratic Force in the Western part of the country.

- **Military Coups:** Since Independence, Uganda has witnessed three successful military coups: Idi Amin's coup which overthrew Obote's first regime in January 1971; a coup by the Military Commission, led by Paulo Muwanga, that removed Godfrey Binaisa's government from power in May 1980; and a coup, led by Bazalio Okello that removed Obote's second regime from power in July 1985.

- **Change of Regimes:** Uganda has had eight different regimes since political independence: Milton Obote's first regime (1962-1971) within which there was an internal change in leadership when Edward Mutesa, who had served as a ceremonial President since 1963, was replaced by Obote, who subsequently promoted himself from the position of the Prime Minister to that of the executive President, following the constitutional crisis of 1966; Amin's regime (1971-April 1979); Yusufu Lule's regime (April-June 1979); Godfrey Binaisa's regime (June 1979-May 1980); Paulo Muwanga's regime (May-December 1980); Obote's second regime (December 1980-July 1985); Tito Okello's regime (July 1985-January 1986); and Yoweri Museveni's regime (January 1986 to the present).

- **Breakdown of Law and Order**: Problems of internal security in Uganda first became serious during the later years of Obote's first regime. Following the 1966 constitutional crisis in Uganda, there were many arrests and detentions without trial of elements suspected of being anti-government. This practice became even worse during Amin's leadership, for, most of the suspected elements were killed rather than detained. Following Amin's overthrow, there was insecurity in almost every part of Uganda: several thousands of people fled into neighboring countries in fear of reprisals. In and around the capital city of Kampala murders, armed robberies, and rapes became rampant. Given Amin's legacy and having

11

inherited undisciplined and poorly trained security forces, Obote's second regime failed to improve the internal security situation in Uganda. Okello's regime, which replaced that of Obote, did not improve the situation either, and it was itself removed by Museveni's NRA guerrilla force. Since Museveni took over the government in 1986, internal security has improved in most of the country, except in those parts of the north where guerrilla warfare is taking place.

- **External Intervention:** Since political independence in 1962, Uganda has experienced three major external interventions: (i) under the conviction that Obote's leadership was assisting rebels against its government, Zaire bombed villages in north-western Uganda in May 1965; (ii) in September 1972, the Tanzanian-based Ugandan exiles invaded Uganda; and (iii) following Amin's invasion of Tanzania in October 1978, Tanzanian troops together with Ugandan exiles waged a war against Uganda, leading ultimately to a forceful removal of Amin's military regime from power in April 1979.

- **Economic Dislocations:** Uganda's economy at independence was characterized by two main types of dependence (i) the country's dependence on Britain for both

12

export and import trade; and (ii) dependence on two cash-crops--coffee and cotton-—which accounted for over 80 percent of the country's exports. As well, Uganda's political economy was characterized by a variety of economic inequalities: (i) at the national level, inequalities existed between European and Asian commercial strata as well as African political and economic elites, on the one hand, and African peasants and workers on the other; (ii) at the local level, inequalities existed between the emergent local politicians and chiefs on the one hand and the governed on the other; and (iii) regional economic disparities existed between southern and northern Uganda, since the former took a lead in commercial, industrial, and educational development as well as in cash-crop production. This economic structure remained essentially unchanged throughout the 1960s.

Following Amin's coup of January 1971, however, Uganda's economy was dislocated even further. Amin was responsible for enormous dislocation of the economy in a number of ways, including:(i) expulsion of Asian and European commercial strata and the subsequent mismanagement of their abandoned properties and businesses by Amin's soldiers who inherited them; (ii) high military expenditure which exhausted the country's limited foreign reserves, thus leaving no money to import basic essentials such as hoes, medical and educational supplies; and (iii) printing money out of proportion to economic productivity, which led to an inflationary spiral.

Uganda continued to suffer from economic dislocations inherited from Amin's legacy since, among other things, the immediate post-Amin political leaders were more preoccupied with struggles for power rather than rehabilitating the country's economic woes.

Organization of the Study

The study falls into eight chapters. Chapter two presents an overview of the historical development of Uganda from the pre-colonial period to independence, focusing on politicization of socio-economic, religious, and regional cleavages. The main purpose of this chapter is to familiarize the reader with basic information about Uganda and, in so doing, to provide a basis for subsequent chapters.

Chapter three is concerned with the impact of institutional development on political order and disorder in Uganda. Attention is paid to two national institutions, namely political parties and the independence constitution, and the impact of their development on political disorder in Uganda.

Chapter four discusses the main constraints on political order, which were inherited from the colonial administration, and analyses the successes and failures of Obote's first leadership (1962-1971) in dealing with those constraints. As well, the chapter discusses the extent to which Obote's first leadership dealt with other sources of constraints on political order, including: lack of popular legitimacy on the part of political leadership; leadership's identification with sectional politics; leadership's failure to establish effective control over the military; and leadership's mismanagement of the economy.

Chapter five examines Amin's dictatorial rule in Uganda by focusing, first, on the conditions under which this leadership emerged, second, on the circumstances under which it persisted despite its colossal brutality against the wider Ugandan society and, finally, on the extent to which this leadership contributed to both political and economic decay.

Chapter six discusses post-Amin regimes by evaluating their respective Performances on the basis of three types of government policies: (i) economic, mainly concerned with the extent to which these regimes attempted to rehabilitate the country's economy; (ii) internal security, examining the efforts made by these regimes to re-establish political order and security in the country; and (iii) administrative, analyzing the manner in which each of these regimes dealt with questions of legitimacy and factional politics.

Chapter seven discusses the performance of Museveni's government, using the same three criteria mentioned above.

The final section, which constitutes chapter eight, summarizes the Conclusions, drawn from the study as a whole, and provides policy recommendations.

CHAPTER II

INITIAL SOURCES OF POLITICAL DISORDER IN UGANDA

Theories of modernization assert that communalism is the main source of constraints on political order and political cohesion in ethnically differentiated societies of developing countries, and that processes of modernization are a solution to such constraints [1]. The above assertions notwithstanding, evidence drawn from Uganda indicates that far from promoting political order and/or cohesion, elements of modernization have actually led to a variety of constraints on political order in that country. In particular, uneven colonial penetration, which allowed for differential access to elements of modernization (modern economy, modern education, modern infrastructures, and the like) to various sub-national groups in Uganda, provoked both competition and conflict among them. This, in turn, led to recurrent sources of political disorder in the country [2].

The concern here is to identify, on the one hand, the main features of socio-political structures in pre-colonial Uganda and, on the other, to examine the extent to which these structures were later transformed during the colonial period, leading to new forms of social stratification and cultural identity.

Pre-colonial Societies

On the basis of insights drawn from anthropological studies of African traditional political systems [3], political structures in pre-colonial Uganda may broadly be divided into two categories: (i) **segmentary systems**, comprising pre-colonial societies in Northern, Eastern, and, to a limited extent, Western Uganda; and (ii) **centralized systems**, comprising pre-colonial societies in Southern and most of Western Uganda.

- Segmentary societies were composed of different subgroups (clans) who shared a common culture and spoke a common language, but were otherwise independent of one another in their socio-political activities. Each clan had its own political leaders, chosen by elders from among themselves, who were responsible for a variety of functions, including: distribution of land among families that constituted the clan, resolving conflicts within the clans and, quite occasionally, holding meetings with neighboring clan leaders to discuss matters of mutual interest. Based mainly on a communal mode of production, a clear sexual division of labor occurred within each household of the clan. Men cleared new lands and defended the clan against enemies. Women grew

18

crops, prepared meals, and took care of children and the elderly. The overall control of the household property was in the hands of the household head, usually a man.

- Centralized societies, on the other hand, were composed of different clans, which were held together by the institution of Kingship that was hereditary. All clans owed their allegiance to a single authority at the centre of the polity, and it was this authority that appointed lower authorities, which were responsible for the administration of the society as a whole. At least this was generally the case in the pre-colonial Kingdoms of Southern and Western Uganda, namely Buganda, Bunyoro, and Ankole [4]. However, some differences existed among these kingdoms in regard to levels of their internal centralization and integration.

At the advent of colonial rule, Buganda was the most highly centralized of these Kingdoms. Heading the Kingdom was the Kabaka (King) who had power to make war, to tax his subjects, who numbered more than a million, to settle disputes, to appoint chiefs and, with the help of clan leaders (Bataka), to allocate land. Below the Kabaka was a three tier-hierarchy of chiefs -- the County

(Saza) chiefs, the Sub-county (Gombolola) chiefs, and the Parish (Miluka) chiefs.

Integration within the kingdom was promoted by at least three factors: (i) a network of roads that radiated from the royal capital at Mengo to all corners of the Kingdom on the basis of which the Kabaka was able to control his chiefs who, in turn, were able to assert control over their respective areas; (ii) the absence of a rigid, caste-defined social structure in the Bugandan society; and (iii) the availability of equal opportunities for individual social mobility since the Kabaka recruited his chiefs mainly on the basis of merit, thereby enabling people from a humble background to constitute part of his administration [5].

The Kingdom of Bunyoro, by contrast, was internally divided on a caste basis. The pastoral Babito constituted the ruling caste while the agriculturalist Bairu, who formed the overwhelming majority within the kingdom, were commoners. The Omukama (king) of Bunyoro ruled indirectly through a group of regional chiefs whom he appointed from among the Babito to serve as administrative heads of the various regions into which the Kingdom was divided.
Lacking a network of communications, as existed in Buganda, the Omukama had little control over his regional chiefs some of whom

wielded so much power that they could easily defy the King with impunity [6].

The smaller Kingdom of Ankole was also internally divided on a rigid, caste-defined basis. The pastoral Bahima and the agriculturalist Bairu constituted the ruling caste and commoners, respectively. The Omugabe (King) of Ankole appointed his chiefs (who usually were men) from the ruling caste on the basis of the number of cattle possessed by potential candidates, for, as an expert on that kingdom has rightly observed, "the main occupation of the rulers and the yardstick of society's wealth was cattle and the administrative system was built around this" [7].

Although centralized societies in pre-colonial Uganda were essentially based on a feudal mode of production [8], differences existed in the internal economies of these societies. In the Kingdoms of Bunyoro and Ankole, where caste differentiation existed, the Bairu (commoners) were reduced to the status of serfs to serve the interests of the ruling aristocracy, without being given opportunities for upward social mobility. In the Kingdom of Buganda, on the other hand, where the merit system in the appointment of chiefs existed, a person of peasant origin could be

21

elevated to be part of the ruling aristocracy on the basis of personal performance [9].

Interaction among and between these two types of pre-colonial societies was mainly through trade and, occasionally, through conflict. Interaction through conflict was mainly provoked by expansionist ambitions on the part of the larger kingdoms of Bunyoro and Buganda. At the height of its power, between the 17th and 18th centuries, Bunyoro was both the commercial and political centre of pre-colonial Uganda. During this period, Bunyoro received tribute from its neighbors, including Buganda, over which it exercised political hegemony. By the19th century, however, Buganda had taken over the leadership.

Through its trade with Arabs from the East African Coast, Buganda acquired a more advanced technology in warfare, especially gunfire, which it used to expand its influence over the neighboring societies. As will be indicated in the next section, it was during this period that colonial rule was declared over Uganda, with Buganda taking an upper hand in almost every colonial innovation.

Politicization of Ethnic Cleavages

The contemporary Ugandan state was introduced by the British colonial power at the turn of the century [10]. The initial political institutions of the colonial state, namely local governments, were developed to coincide with boundaries already separating the pre-colonial ethnic groups, discussed in the preceding section. However, preferential treatment was accorded to different local governments during the colonial period, thereby politicizing ethnic cleavages on which these local administrative institutions were primarily based.

Having found the kingdom of Buganda at the height of its power, the British decided, first, to declare a protectorate over it, in 1893, and then later to make it a base for the expansion of colonial rule over the rest of Uganda. The Baganda, for their part, not only collaborated with the colonial power in the annexation of the Kingdom of Bunyoro, which had resisted the imposition of colonial rule over it, but they also served as agents of colonial power in transplanting Kiganda political institutions to other areas, as local governments were being set up. For these and other related services to the colonial power, the Baganda became the most favored ethnic group throughout the colonial period [11]. David

Apter has provided another explanation, which is no less significant than the ones given above, for Buganda's favored position during the colonial period:

> Whether or not their views were correct, missionaries and administrators saw in the institutions of the Buganda Kingdom familiar instruments of government. This led to collaboration with the Baganda which, if it lacked intimacy, nevertheless gave character and strength to later administrative policy. The Baganda became the most favored nation [12].

Whatever the rationale, the preferential treatment accorded to Buganda during the colonial period became one of the main factors that contributed to subsequent political disorder in Uganda, as part of the discussion below will indicate.

The Buganda Agreement of 1900, signed by a representative of the British government (Sir Harry Johnston) and the leading chiefs of Buganda, established a quasi-diplomatic relationship between the imperial power and the Buganda government, on the basis of which the latter was to enjoy a measure of administrative autonomy. The same agreement granted additional concessions to Buganda. The chiefs and notables of Buganda were provided with the right to own private estates, which together amounted to half the land in the entire Kingdom. As well, Buganda was allocated part of Bunyoro's

Territory that later became a source of a constitutional crisis both during and after colonial rule [13].

The kingdoms of Western Uganda were less favored in comparison with Buganda. Although their hereditary rulers were recognized by the colonial power, the appointment of their subordinate chiefs became a function of the colonial government and not of the indigenous rulers. These chiefs, moreover, were allowed to acquire land, the use of which terminated at the end of their term in office. Finally, some pre-colonial institutions in these Kingdoms were gradually replaced by Kiganda-type institutions, with which colonial officials were more familiar.

Least favored of all local governments were those developed by grouping clans of segmentary societies that shared a common cultural identity. Since these lacked central authority, the colonial power employed Baganda agents, first, to introduce Kigada-type centralized institutions and then, later, to carry out administrative functions in these local governments. Other than allowing senior chiefs in these new local governments (who were mostly Baganda agents) to acquire freehold land, no further concessions were made to these non-kingdom local governments (commonly known as districts).

In addition to the above, two other important factors worked in favor of Buganda in comparison with all other parts of the country. First, European penetration into Uganda was through Buganda. Both missionaries and colonial rulers, who were responsible for education and administration respectively, concentrated their initial efforts on Buganda before turning to other parts of the country, with the result that the earliest schools, hospitals, and indeed the headquarters of the colonial government itself were all built in Buganda. And second, patterns of economic growth and organization in Uganda also started in Buganda before spreading to other parts. The initial cash crops, cotton and coffee, that were introduced in Uganda by the colonial government, were first grown in Buganda before they were experimented with elsewhere, and industries, together with infrastructures that were associated with the processing and marketing of those crops, were concentrated in Buganda.

Because of this privileged position, acquired almost incidentally by Buganda, Uganda's political history right from the early years of colonial rule up to independence was dominated by a dialectic: (i) a desire of the Kingdoms of western Uganda as well as districts to set a limit to the continuation of Buganda's special status within

Ugandan politics; and (ii) Buganda's concerted efforts to maintain its superior position within Uganda at whatever cost.

Politicization of Social and Regional Cleavages

Having established a system of local government through which colonial rule could be exercised at the grassroots level, the colonial government proceeded to reorganize the economy of Uganda, aiming at two main goals: (i) to turn Uganda into a producer of raw materials for metropolitan manufacturing industries; and (ii) to make the Ugandan colony self-financing.

By the early 1930s, at least three major policies had been introduced to achieve these goals. First, two main cash crops (cotton and coffee) had been introduced in Uganda, and people in selected areas were required to divide their time in producing food crops for their own consumption and export crops for British industry. Second, a poll tax was imposed by the colonial state whereby every adult male in Uganda was required either to pay annual tax in cash or to provide one month's labor to the colonial state, by working on state-run projects such as roads, health centers, government buildings and the like [14].

Local chiefs, for their part, were required to exert direct pressure on their subjects, first, to produce export crops in quantities that would sustain the requirements of British industries and, second, to pay poll tax on time.

And finally, with the expansion of the commercial economy in Uganda, the colonial government encouraged the establishment of credit systems by inviting British-based banks to open branches in Uganda [15]. As well, European and Asian traders, manufacturers, and financiers were encouraged to establish businesses in Uganda, including hire-purchase services, export-import trade, insurance, and retail trade [16].

Overall, there was a three-fold impact of the new colonial economic order on Ugandan society. First, most of the local industries that had existed in pre-colonial Uganda were gradually destroyed as colonial economic innovations spread throughout the country. During the pre-colonial period, artisans in the Kingdoms of Ankole and Bunyoro had excelled in the production of iron hoes, carpentry, and pottery. Baganda artisans, for their part, were manufacturing such products as sandals, bark cloth, and soap. However, with the introduction of the colonial economy, based essentially on export-import trade, even the hoe -- the basic tool in a peasant agricultural economy - was imported from Britain.

Instead of encouraging the growth of indigenous industries, the colonial government supported the establishment of a few new industries aimed at: (i) servicing the export-import trade, and (ii) meeting the immediate needs of foreigners in the country. Cotton ginneries and coffee processing works were established to reduce costs of transporting these cash crops abroad. Bakeries, butcheries, and plants for producing soft drinks, ice cream, beer, and the like, were established to meet the consumption needs of foreign residents.

The second impact of the colonial economic order was the integration of Uganda into the world economy as a producer of raw materials for, and a consumer of manufactured products from, the developed economies, and in particular Britain. The "cotton famine" in the Manchester textile industry and Britain's intent to avoid being over-dependent on coffee supplies from the US-dominated South American market, led the British government to exert pressure on its tropical colonies to concentrate on the production of those two major crops.

After extending a railway line from the East African coast to the interior, linking Uganda to Britain through the Indian Ocean, cotton and coffee were made the leading export commodities of Uganda, with the result that by the end of colonial rule these two crops alone accounted for more than 80 percent of Uganda's exports earnings. Britain was not only the main outlet of Uganda's exports. It was also the main source of Uganda's imports. In other words, Uganda's economy not only became dependent on two primary products which it exported to Britain; it also became dependent on Britain for its imports, thus putting Britain in a position to direct and condition Uganda's economy in a way that would meet some of British essential economic interests [17].

Finally, the colonial economy promoted some new types of socio-economic inequalities in Ugandan society. Pre-colonial Buganda chiefs were converted into a class of landlords. In their new dual capacity as landlords and rulers, these chiefs stripped away from their tenant-subjects much of their surplus produce in the form of rent. Elsewhere local chiefs were provided with freehold land that, in addition to regular salaries, raised their economic status substantially above that of their subjects. One result was that in segmentary societies, where privileged chieftainship never existed during the pre-colonial period, the newly introduced polarization between leaders and the led provoked a measure of resentment [18].

Socio-economic inequalities also developed at both the national and regional levels. While southern Uganda, especially Buganda and its neighboring areas, monopolized the production of export crops, northern Uganda was developed essentially as a labor reserve from which soldiers, police, and workers could be recruited as needed [19].

Moreover, Kampala and Jinja, both located in southern Uganda, were developed as commercial and industrial centers, respectively, while no comparable projects were developed in northern Uganda.

At the national level, inequalities existed between foreign interests and Africans, on the one hand, and among Africans themselves, on the other.

At the apex were the Europeans who held a commanding position in power, status, and wealth. Below the Europeans were the Asians, who acquired financial support from both the colonial state and the credit institutions to establish a variety of businesses, including cotton ginning, retail trade, and serving as middlemen between cash crop producers and cash crop exporters.

Below the Asians, but at the top of the African economic ladder, were African economic elites, mainly found in Buganda, who owned the new plantations of export crops. These included Baganda chiefs and notables who, by the Buganda Agreement of 1900, had acquired large private estates, parts of which were rented to peasants and other parts turned into plantations for cotton and coffee.

Below these was a new group of Africans who, through the acquisition of some degree of Western education, had qualified for some jobs within the colonial state. These included clerks in public bureaucracies, teachers, clergy, interpreters, and a variety of junior staff technicians.

At the bottom of this economic hierarchy were the peasants, the majority of whom were poor, illiterate and locked in rural areas primarily as subsistence producers [20].

Another factor that has had an influence on the political history of Uganda is religion. For, as will be indicated below, religious

32

cleavages were also politicised during the colonial period, leading ultimately to religious competition and conflict. And, since modern education was introduced in Uganda by missionaries, its development and distribution was influenced by the politicization of religious cleavages. It is to the development of religion and education in Uganda that I will now turn.

Politicization of Religious Cleavages

Foreign religions-- Islam and Christianity-- were both introduced in Uganda before colonial rule. Islam was introduced by Arab traders from the East African coast, which arrived in Buganda around 1844. The Anglican Church Missionary Society and the Catholic White Fathers arrived in Buganda in 1877 and 1879, respectively. These three denominations made their initial converts at the Kabaka's Court before penetrating the rest of Buganda society. However, rivalry developed among them and, fearing to lose control over his Kingdom to factions of religious converts, Kabaka Mwanga persecuted all new Christians who refused to renounce their faith [21]. They were burnt alive in 1886 at Namugongo, a few miles from Kampala.

Following this massacre, missionaries were determined to install their future converts in positions of authority and, to that end, they

33

fashioned their own private armies which they used first to depose Kabaka Mwanga in 1889, and then later to defeat the Muslim faction in 1890.

After weakening its common enemies (Mwanga and the Muslims), the Christian community was itself divided along the Catholic-Protestant axis. An armed conflict erupted between these Christian factions in 1892, with the Protestants being backed decisively by the secular power of the Imperial British Eastern African Company which, under Sir (later Lord) Frederick Lugard, had received a mandate from the British government to extend its hold over Buganda.

During the next few years, the British government declared a protectorate over Buganda (1893), and negotiated a settlement with the leading chiefs of that Kingdom (the Buganda Agreement of 1900) under which, among other things, a quota system -- whereby public offices in Buganda were to be allocated on the basis of religious affiliations - was established. According to this settlement, the Kabaka together with two of his three ministers were to be Protestants, the third ministry being reserved for a Catholic. Of twenty county Chiefs of Buganda, ten were to be Protestants, eight Catholics, and two Muslims.

In short, the Buganda Agreement of 1900 established religion as a basis of recruitment into the Buganda administration, thereby eroding the merit system on the basis of which the Kabaka had always recruited his chiefs during the pre-colonial period. With the help of Baganda missionaries and Baganda agents in spreading Christianity and colonial rule respectively, this pattern of using religious criteria in the allocation of public offices was repeated over the greater part of Uganda [22].

Having installed their converts in positions of authority, the missionaries were next concerned with establishing educational institutions through which they could educate and, in so doing, socialize the future leaders of the country.

However, two types of inequalities were associated with the development of the modern educational system in colonial Uganda. First, since modern education was provided mainly by missionary schools, Muslims, who lacked missionaries to build schools for them, were grossly underdeveloped educationally, leading them to enter the modern sector through trade, mainly as butchers and taxi-drivers. Their Christian counterparts, on the other hand, found their way into the modern sector as administrators and, ultimately, as

35

politicians. Second, missionary schools themselves were not evenly distributed throughout the country. In particular, the northern part of Uganda which was least penetrated by missionaries during most of the colonial period remained the least developed educationally in comparison with other regions in the country [23].

The unequal distribution of benefits that was associated with the introduction of foreign religions and modern education, divided Ugandan society in at least two further ways. First, the preference that colonial agents gave to Protestants led to the development of what later came to be known as the "Protestant establishment" in Uganda [24]. This caused resentment among other religious denominations [25], more particularly among Catholics, whose efforts to obtain full recognition within Ugandan politics ultimately culminated in the formation of a "Catholic" political party in 1956 -- the Democratic Party - intended primarily to redress Catholic grievances [26]. And second, the unequal distribution of educational facilities among geographical regions in Uganda caused resentment among the least educated Northerners, who complained to the colonial government that senior posts in their native administration were filled with "foreigners" and demanded that their children should be well-educated in order for them to provide future leadership in their own area [27].

CONCLUSION

Overall, most elements of modernization which were introduced in Uganda during the colonial period or, more specifically, the colonial policies that were associated with the introduction of these elements, divided Ugandan society in at least four ways. In the first instance, they gave Buganda a lead in socio-economic and political growth which, in turn, created Baganda ascendancy in administrative and economic status at the expense of other groups in the country, causing resentment against the Baganda on both counts [28].

Second, regional inequalities developed between northern and southern Uganda, since the latter attained an upper hand over the former in both education and the modern economy.

Third, at the local level, and more particularly in the districts of Bugisu and Toro, socio-economic and political inequalities developed between the mountain ethnic groups -- the Bamba and Bakonjo of Mount Ruenzori and the Sebei of Mount Elgon -- and the larger ethnic groups to which they had been incorporated, the Batoro and Bagisu, respectively, in regard to: (i) availability of educational facilities; (ii) appointment opportunities to local government jobs, and (iii) availability of socio-economic development projects. These inequalities ultimately led the underprivileged mountain ethnic groups to resort to violence on the eve of Uganda's independence.

And finally, the development of modern education was primarily undertaken by religious denominations and, given the politicization of religious cleavages discussed above, the main national political parties that competed for leadership at independence were divided along religious lines. This division deprived Uganda of the opportunity to develop a strong and representative nationalist party, like TANU in neighboring Tanganyika, capable of securing political dominance at independence. Instead, Ugandan political parties have been characterized by intra-party dissensions and inter-party fluidity during most of the post-colonial period.

Thus, contrary to theories of modernization, asserting that elements of modernization are vital in promoting political order and cohesion in developing countries, the preceding discussion suggests that the roots of ethnic competition and conflicts, which have partly impeded political order and cohesion in Uganda, should be sought in differential access to certain elements of modernization which the colonial government allowed to various sub-national groups in that country, thereby politicizing regional, religious, and ethnic cleavages.

NOTES

[1] See especially: James Coleman and Gabriel Almond (eds), <u>The Politics of Developing Areas</u>, Princeton, Princeton University Press, 1960; Clifford Geertz (ed), <u>Old Societies and New States: The Quest for Modernity in Asia and Africa</u>, New York, Free Press, 1958; and Daniel Lerner, <u>The Passing of the Traditional Society</u>: <u>Modernization of the Middle East</u>, Glencoe, The Free Press, 1958.

[2] Political disorder is here defined in terms of social conflict, political violence and high levels of instability.

[3] See especially M. Fortes and E. Evans-Prichard (eds.), <u>African Political Systems</u>, London, Oxford University Press, 1940; and S. N. Eisenstadt, "Primitive Political Systems: A Preliminary Comparative Analysis," <u>American Anthropologist,</u> 61(1959) pp.200-220. For a general review of this earlier scholarship on African traditional political systems, see Christian Potholm (ed), <u>The Theory and Practice of African Politics</u>, Englewood Cliffs, Prentice-Hall, 1979, pp.3-33.

[4] At the advent of colonial rule, there were four kingdoms in Uganda: Ankole, Buganda, Bunyoro, and Toro. However, the

Kingdom of Toro had been part of the larger kingdom of Bunyoro until the late 19th century when the colonial agent, Lord Lugard, helped a faction that was attempting to secede from Bunyoro to form a separate kingdom of Toro. In all essentials, therefore, Toro did not exist as a separate kingdom in pre-colonial Uganda. For a historical development of the kingdom of Toro, see Kenneth Ingham, The Kingdom of Toro in Uganda, London, Oxford University Press, 1975.

[5] For a detailed account on pre-colonial Buganda, see especially M. S. Kiwanuka, A History of Buganda, London, Longmans, 1971.

[6] For an account on pre-colonial Bunyoro, see John Beatie, Bunyoro: An African Kingdom, New York, Holt, Rinehart and Winston, 1960; and his The Nyoro State, Oxford University Press, 1971.

[7] Samwiri Karugire, A Political History of Uganda, Nairobi, Heinemann Educational Books, 1980, P.24. For a more detailed account on pre-colonial Ankole, see Samwiri Karugire, A History of Ankole in Western Uganda to 1896, London, Oxford University Press, 1971.

[8] A feudal relation is here defined simply as obligatory provision of services and tribute by the producers to the ruling aristocracy in return for security and protection. For a discussion of this concept along these lines in relation to the Ugandan pre-colonial Kingdoms, see especially: Mahmood Mamdani, Politics and Class Formation in Uganda, London,_Heinemann, 1976, pp.23-28; and D.Wadada Nabudere, Imperialism and Revolution in Uganda, London, Onyx Press, 1980, pp.15-20.

[9] The Kabaka appointed his chiefs from among the pages on the basis of their performances while serving at his court. The selection of pages to serve at the Kabaka's court was not usually based on personal background.

[10] A state as a political form of human organization existed in pre-colonial Ugandan societies, especially among the centralized systems discussed above. What concerns me here, however, is the historical development of the contemporary sovereign territorial unit known as the Ugandan state.

[11] See especially, Anthony Low and Cranford Pratt, Buganda and British Overrule 1900-1955: Two Studies, London, Oxford University Press, 1960.

[12] David Apter, The Political Kingdom in Uganda: A Study of Bureaucratic Nationalism, Princeton, Princeton University Press, 1961, p64.

[13] For a detailed account of this agreement, see especially, Anthony Low, "The Making and Implementation of the Uganda Agreement of 1900", in Pratt and Low, Buganda and British Overrule, pp.3-137; and G.N.Uzoigwe, "The Agreement States and the Making of Uganda: Buganda", in G. N. Uzoigwe (ed), Uganda: The Dilemma of Nationhood, New York, NOK Publishers International, 1982, pp.57-93. As will be discussed in some detail in later chapters, the colonial government gave Buganda part of Bunyoro's territory as a reward for its help in the annexation of Bunyoro, which had resisted colonial rule. Bunyoro's demand for the return of this territory throughout the colonial period turned into the longest constitutional problem in Uganda's modern history.

[14] During the colonial period women, elderly males, and disabled adult males were exempted from paying poll tax. The latter two

groups were considered unfit to provide manual labor by which poll tax was usually earned. Women on the other hand were left to take care of children and the bulk of other domestic services.

[15] The National Bank of India, whose headquarters were in Britain, opened its first branch in Uganda in 1906. The Standard Bank and Barclays Bank later also opened branches in Uganda.

[16] For a detailed account on European and Asian businesses in Uganda, see especially Jan Jorgensen, Uganda: A Modern History, New York, St. Martin's Press, 1981,pp.134-175; and M.Mamdani, Politics and Class Formation in Uganda, pp.65-119.

[17] For a discussion of Uganda's economic dependence on Britain, see especially: Mahmood Mamdani, Imperialism and Fascism in Uganda, Nairobi, Heinemann Educational Books, 1983; and E.A. Brett, Colonialism and Underdevelopment in East Africa: The Politics of Economic Change, 1919-39, London, Heinemann, 1973,pp.237-265.

[18] See especially Tarsis Kabwegyere, The Politics of State Formation: The Nature and Effects of Colonialism in Uganda, Nairobi, East African Literature Bureau, 1974, pp.79-85.

[19] See especially: H. Moyse-Bartlett, The King's African Rifles, Aldershot, Gale and Polden, 1956; and E.F. Whitehead, "A Short History of Uganda Military Units Formed During World War II", Uganda Journal, 14(March 1950) pp.1-14.

[20] It is important to note that socio-economic strata especially among Africans were not as clear-cut as indicated above. There were some overlaps. Among the peasants, for example, some were relatively poorer than others, depending upon location. Peasants in Buganda were generally better off than other peasants in the rest of southern Uganda who, in turn, were better off than peasants in the north.

[21] At least three main factors seem to have influenced Mwanga's decision to single out Christian converts for persecution at this point in time. First, unlike their Muslim rivals who had both taught their religion and traded in firearms that gave Buganda a superior warfare technology in comparison with its neighbors, Christian missionaries insisted on teaching religion only which, in the judgment of the Kabaka, devalued their utility to the kingdom of Buganda. Second, Muslims took every opportunity to discredit the Christian missionaries before the Kabaka in order to protect their

interests in Buganda, which were being challenged by the new European-based religious factions. And finally, Christian converts (including pages in the Kabaka's Court and Chiefs) were gradually becoming impatient with some aspects of the unquestionable power of the Kabaka, which gradually became incompatible with their newly-acquired religious faith, leading the Kabaka to consider their attitudes as a source of insubordination within his kingdom. See especially Karugire, A Political History of Uganda, pp.62-70.

[22] In the peripheral kingdoms of Ankole, Bunyoro, and Toro, the King together with his Prime Minister were always Protestants. In non-kingdom districts, the highest post of Secretary-General was usually occupied by a Protestant. Meanwhile, the percentage of Catholics, both in Buganda and Uganda as a whole, was higher than that of Protestants. See F. B. Welbourn, Religion and Politics in Uganda 1952-1962, Nairobi, East African Publishing House, 1965.

[23] By 1920 the distribution of elementary schools according to the four major administrative regions in Uganda was as follows: 328 in Buganda, 34 in Western Province, 24 in Eastern Province, and none in Northern Province. Twenty years later (1940), the distribution of secondary schools was as follows: 3 in Buganda, 2

in Western Province, 2 in Eastern Province and none in Northern Province. In fact a secondary school in Northern Province was not established until 1955. For these statistics and their sources, see Kabwegyere, The Politics of State Formation, pp.179-191.

[24] For a detailed account of the Protestant establishment in Uganda, see especially Kathleen Lockard, "Politics and Religion in Independent Uganda: Movement Toward Secularization", in James Scarritt (ed), Analysing Political Change in Africa: Application of a New Multidimensional Framework, Boulder, Westview Press, 1980, pp.40-73. Basically, the Protestant establishment in Uganda implied that the political power which accrued to Protestants was not justified by the latter's numerical strength in the country, especially as compared with Catholics.

[25] For an analysis of these resentments during the colonial period, see especially James Katorobo, Education for Public Service in Uganda, New York, Vantage Press, 1982, pp.19-24.

[26] See especially Anthony Low, Political Parties in Uganda 1949-1962, London, Athlone Press, 1962.

[27] See parts of the report by the Provincial Commissioner for Northern Province, A.Warner, reproduced by Kabwegyere, The Politics of State Formation P.180. The "foreigners" referred to above were Ugandans recruited from outside northern Uganda, especially from Buganda, to carry out administrative functions since Northerners lacked educated elites to fill them up.

[28] The study done by Nelson Kasfir indicates that by Uganda's independence, the percentage of Baganda in the higher public service of Uganda was 46.9. Nelson Kasfir, The Shrinking Political Arena: Participation and Ethnicity in African Politics, With a Case Study of Uganda, Berkeley, University of California Press, 1976, Table 4, P.186.

CHAPTER III

DEVERLOPMENT OF EARLY INSTITUTIONS

Constraints on political order in Uganda arose not only from the development of colonial political structures, discussed in the previous chapter, but also from the development of two national political institutions: political parties and the Independence Constitution, both of which involved the active participation of indigenous Ugandans.

Although developed within the framework of the colonial state, these two types of political institutions were expected to provide a firm foundation on the basis of which cooperation and accommodation among sub-national groups in Uganda could be promoted prior to political independence [1].

The main purpose of this chapter is to examine some of the factors that led to the failure of these institutions to attain the objectives expected of them and, in so doing, to identify the main constraints on political order in Uganda that arose from the development of these two institutions.

Development of Early National Political Parties.

In the 1960s, much of the literature on developing countries was characterized by theorizing on the vital role that political parties could play in promoting political order and cohesion in these countries [2]. However, the extent to which political parties could achieve these objectives depended on at least two main factors: (i) the capability of these political parties to forge a strong sense of national identity among sub-national groups, which would supersede the more limited parochial loyalties, at least in relation to important political matters [3]; and (ii) the degree to which leaders of these political parties were committed to acquiring popular legitimacy for their parties [4].

In Uganda, however, neither of these requirements was fulfilled by any of the political parties that developed in that country. The Ugandan political elites failed to develop a well-structured nationalist movement on the basis of which a broad national popular support could be mobilized prior to independence.

At least three main reasons seem to have been responsible for that failure: (i) the fact that these elites knew that Uganda was soon going to be self-governing [5]; (ii) the general absence of strong national-oriented political grievances, capable of uniting indigenous Ugandans into a national movement against colonial rule [6]; and (iii) the Ugandan colonial social structure in which both ethnic and religious cleavages had been politicized, by the colonial state, to fight each other as indicated in the preceding chapter. It is against this background that I will now discuss the development of Ugandan political parties.

The Uganda National Congress (UNC)

The UNC, the first national party to be established in Uganda, was created in 1952 by a Muganda political activist, Ignatius Musazi [7]. It derived its name from the Indian National Congress (INC), which had previously led India to political independence [8]. Unlike its counterpart in India, however, the UNC as long as it lasted neither acquired a national appeal nor did it lead Uganda to political independence, mainly because of the problems that accompanied its birth to which I will now turn.

In the attempt to justify its claim as a nationalist political party, and in the absence of stronger nation-wide political grievances on the basis of which it could mobilize broad popular political support, the UNC became critical of ethnic-based local governments in Uganda, and more particularly of Buganda, which enjoyed a special status among these local governments. The consequences of this policy for the UNC were two-fold: (i) it was resented by the government of Buganda because of its open criticism of the monarchy; and (ii) having been founded in Buganda, a region that had enjoyed a privileged position throughout the colonial period, the UNC was mistrusted in other regions in the country which were not sure of its intentions.

Faced with these problems, the UNC abandoned its original policy and sought to acquire political support outside Buganda by exploiting local issues of political discontent, on a district by district basis. It recruited some members by supporting political elements that were opposed to the colonial government's policy of reserving land in the district of Toro for the Queen Elizabeth National Park. In the district of Bugisu the UNC aligned with members of the Bugisu Coffee Union who had had a long battle with the colonial government over the management of that union. Finally, the UNC supported those elements that were discontented with the colonial government's refusal to recognize the small hereditary chieftainships that existed in Busoga. In most other parts of Uganda where local discontents were not so severe as to attract the attention of the UNC's leadership, it neither secured support nor recruited membership.

In the kingdom of Buganda, the UNC sought to acquire support by rallying together with most Baganda in the agitation for the release of their Kabaka from exile during the period 1953-1955. Although the government of Buganda rewarded the UNC's loyalty by allowing some of its members to represent Buganda in the Legislative Council, this favor was short-lived, for, in 1958 the Buganda government refused not only to be represented in the national Legislature, but it also outlawed political parties in Buganda [9].

Lacking both a political ideology and clear-cut goals, other than the slogan "Independence now", and having lost its political base in the Ugandan Legislature, the UNC could no longer hold together. It split into two factions in 1958: one led by Milton Obote, which drew most of its support from the northern and eastern parts of uganda; and the other led by Joseph Kiwanuka and Dr. B.N. Kunuka, whose membership was drawn mainly from Buganda. While the latter faction gradually disappeared into obscurity in the early 1960s, the former merged with another party, the Uganda People's Union (UPU) that had been founded in 1958 by non-Ganda African members of the LEGCO, to form the Uganda People's Congress, which I will discuss later in this chapter. I will now turn to the discussion of the second national party to be developed in Uganda.

The Democratic Party (DP)

The DP was formed in 1956 for two main reasons:(i) to redress Catholic grievances in Uganda [10]; and (ii) to serve as a counterforce to the UNC, which not only was dominated by Protestants both in leadership and membership, but also had been branded as a communist party by some Catholic church leaders in Uganda [11]. In all essentials, therefore, the DP was a Catholic party par excellence, organized by a coalition of the Catholic church, Catholic teachers and priests, and other Catholic interests at both the local and national levels. I will first discuss its origin and then examine some of the problems it faced as a national party.

Following the return of the Kabaka of Buganda from exile in 1955, the Buganda Lukiiko was composed of elected members and the Kabaka's appointees. Of the former, the majority were Catholics, because the latter is a dominant religion in Buganda. Matayo Mugwanya, who was a Catholic and had been a treasurer on the previous Buganda government, was nominated for the position of the prime minister [12]. Pre-election estimates suggested that Mugwanya would win the election. Realizing this, the Kabaka changed his nominees in the Lukiiko and appointed new ones whom he instructed not to vote for Mugwanya, primarily because the latter was a Catholic. As it turned out, Mugwanya lost the election to Michael Kintu, who was a Protestant, by a margin of four votes [13].

Having lost the premiership, Mugwanya was elected to the Lukiiko by Mawokota county, but the Kabaka refused to approve his election on the grounds that Mugwanya was a member of the East African Legislative council. Meanwhile, out of six ministers on the Kabaka's government in 1955, only one was a Catholic, while one was Muslim and four were Protestants. This distribution may be contrasted with the religious distribution in Buganda at the time, which was 35% Catholics, 28% Protestants, and 14% Muslims [14].

The above evidence seems to indicate the extent to which Catholics were discriminated against in Buganda. When the DP was formed to redress these injustices, Matayo Mugwanya, who had personally suffered most from this discrimination, was elected its President. The stated objective of the DP was:

> to secure proper representation to legislative authorities and governments so that a solid and sound policy is ensured whereby all sections of the community are treated with equal human and political

rights which enable them to achieve ultimate independence in Uganda [15].

Although the DP mobilized political support from Catholics all over the country with a measure of success, it was confronted with a number of problems, especially in the kingdom of Buganda, which ultimately led to its downfall.

Benedicto Kiwanuka, who assumed the party leadership in 1958, lacked tact and patience in dealing with the people of Buganda although he was himself a Muganda. He not only criticized the exclusive benefits that had been accorded to Buganda by the colonial government, but he also demonstrated his opposition to monarchism in Uganda, including the Kabakaship of Buganda. For the Baganda, whose loyalty to their Kabaka prevailed over any other political consideration, Kiwanuka was seen as a major threat to the special status of the kingdom of Buganda. Consequently the Baganda were determined to frustrate Kiwanuka's political ambitions, at least in Buganda. To that end, the government of Buganda appealed to all Baganda to boycott the 1961 general elections.

Although 97% of the Baganda electorate responded to this appeal and refused to vote, 3% of this electorate, who were die-hard

Catholics, went to the polls and voted for the DP, enabling it to win by default 20 of the 21 Buganda seats in the Ugandan Legislature. In addition, the DP won 23 more seats from the rest of the country, and thus formed a clear majority in the Legislature [16]. As a result of these elections, Kiwanuka became the chief Minister in the short period of Uganda's internal self-government.

The majority of the Baganda, however, were soon to regret their decision to boycott the 1961 general elections, for, one of the early statements made by chief Minister Kiwanuka was that he would "soon make the Kabaka of Buganda see sense" [17]. This statement provoked hostile reactions among the Baganda for at least two reasons: (i) Kiwanuka, though chief Minister of Uganda, was both a Catholic and a Muganda peasant (mukopi), a combination which could not earn him any respectable position within the Buganda establishment; and (ii) by challenging the authority of the Kabaka, without whom the Baganda felt that their special identity within an independent Uganda would diminish, Kiwanuka was seen as a great danger to the kingdom of Buganda. Consequently, the Baganda decided to form their own ethnic party called Kabaka Yekka (KY) with the intention of frustrating Kiwanuka's ambitions in Buganda [18].

Within this spirit of Buganda nationalism, the KY mobilized the Buganda electorate so effectively that in the election for the Buganda Lukiiko in February 1962, 90% of the registered voters cast their ballots in its favor, giving it 65 of the 68 Lukiiko seats. Yet, this election was crucial not only in Buganda but in Uganda as a whole, since Buganda's representatives to the national Parliament were to be elected indirectly by the Lukiiko.

Prior to this election, the President of the UPC, Milton Obote, had persuaded the Kabaka of Buganda that a coalition government should be formed between the KY and the UPC after the independence elections of April 1962. Therefore, the UPC had agreed not to contest the Buganda election of February 1962, leaving the DP and the KY the only contestants.

Having been outvoted in Buganda, Kiwanuka and his DP were a spent force, for, when national elections were held in other parts of Uganda in April 1962, the UPC won 37 seats and the DP only 24 [19].In accordance with the pre-election agreement, the UPC and the KY formed a coalition government, and Obote as the Prime Minister chose his cabinet ministers from both parties. It is to the discussion of the development of Obote's UPC that I will now turn.

The Uganda Peoples' Congress (UPC)

The UPC was born out of a merger between the Uganda Peoples' Union (UPU) and Obote's wing of the UNC on March 9, 1960, with Obote as its first President. There were three major policy objectives of the UPC: (i) to attain Uganda's independence as quickly as possible, but through constitutional means; (ii) to uphold the dignity of hereditary rulers in Uganda and other heads of African governments; and (iii) to secure complete unity of the people of Uganda under a stable government [20].

The immediate background to the formation of the UPC was the publication of the Report of the Constitutional Committee [21], which announced major changes in the constitutional development of Uganda. Among these changes were: an increase of African representation on the Legislative Council, the extension of the franchise, and the granting of a responsible government based on elections to be held in March 1961. These proposed reforms posed a serious challenge to the existing political parties, which were required to recruit prospective candidates and to organize new voters within a period of one year. The merger of the UPU and Obote's wing of the UNC to form the UPC seems to have been prompted by this challenge [22].

61

Both the UPU and Obote's wing of the UNC shared one thing in common: they were essentially anti-Buganda parties. While the latter broke away from the old UNC because it was against the old generation of leaders who were mostly Baganda, the former was founded in 1958 by non-Ganda African members of the Ugandan Legislative Council in reaction to: (i) Baganda's previous political dominance in the country, and (ii) the hostility of the Buganda government towards the development of national political parties.

However, both of these parties had their individual problems. The UPU, whose membership never extended beyond the Legislative Council, was primarily a parliamentary party with no roots in society. Its membership was a coalition of political elites drawn from the ethnic-centered local governments, especially of eastern and western Uganda. Obote's wing of the UNC, on the other hand, had established some roots in northern Uganda, where Obote came from, but was weak in other parts of the country. The merger of these two parties therefore resulted in a party that was a coalition of local interests from areas outside Buganda. Hence, from its inception, the UPC inherited three fundamental problems from both its parents: (i) a regional bias against Buganda, which made the party extremely weak in Buganda;(ii) inadequate grass-root popular support, since the party hardly ever established deep roots in the society; and (iii) a failure on the part of party elites to break out of the local framework and establish new bases on a national foundation [23].

The UPC faced external problems as well. The first and most important of these was the question of Buganda's position in an independent Uganda. The challenge which the UPC faced, as a party aspiring to lead the country, was that of redressing the balance of power in Uganda which previously had swung in favor of Buganda, and at the same time to retain Buganda as an integral part of the independent Ugandan state [24].

The second challenge to the UPC involved political conflicts arising from the previous colonial politicization of ethnic cleavages in Uganda. First, the kingdom of Bunyoro could hardly support any political party that was not ready to tackle the question of the lost counties. Second, the mountain ethnic groups, the Bamba and Bakonjo of Mount Rwenzori and the Sebei of Mount Elgon, could only support a party that was sympathetic to their demands for separate districts. The challenge to the UPC was that of resolving the above-mentioned political conflicts without at the same time losing the support of any of the other groups that were involved in

63

those conflicts. Since, however, the above-mentioned were long-term challenges that could hardly be resolved overnight, the manner in which the UPC, as a party of government, handled them both before and after Uganda's independence will be analyzed as the discussion in this study progresses.

At this stage at least two conclusions can be drawn in relation to the development of political parties in Uganda. First, the failure to develop a well-structured nationalist movement prior to Uganda's independence led to the formation of political parties that were weak, lacking in ideology, and with no well-defined national goals. Consequently, none of these parties acquired a measure of legitimacy and/or effectiveness. And second, the previous politicization of cultural cleavages (ethnicity, religion, and regionalism) by the colonial state, contributed further to the failure of the Ugandan political parties to forge a sense of political accommodation among sub-national groups in the country. For, each of these parties made one or the other of these cultural cleavages a basis for its development. I will now turn to the discussion of the Independence Constitution.

Development of Independence Constitution

Particularly vital among various functions of any country's constitution is the one dealing with the distribution of power [25]. In western democracies, the phrase "distribution of power" immediately evokes the classical idea of checks and balances among the three branches of government: executive, legislative, and judicial. Less immediately apparent in western democracies, but particularly crucial in underdeveloped plural societies, is the distribution of power among the state's constituent sub-national groups. For, a failure to balance political power among these groups in an acceptable manner can readily lead to political disorder.

In the discussion of the Ugandan Independence Constitution, particular attention will be paid to the manner in which this constitution distributed political power among sub-national groups in Uganda. First, however, it appears appropriate to look at the immediate background to this constitution.

The Constitutional Committee of 1959:

Throughout the colonial period, the constitution of Uganda was not embodied in a single document but rather existed in separate

65

Orders-in-Council, Royal Instructions, and Ordinances. Although the major function of the Legislative Council was to legislate for Uganda, its powers of legislation were quite limited, since the most important legislative decisions were taken either by the Colonial Office or by the Governor, both having had the powers to reserve certain bills and to disallow others passed by the Legislative Council [26]. This was the background to Governor Crawford's promise to the Legislative Council in 1958 that, with the permission of Her Majesty's Government, he was going to appoint a Constitutional Committee to deal with the procedures for the national direct elections that were scheduled to take place in Uganda in 1961. The terms of reference of this Constitutional Committee were later announced to the Legislative Council by the Chief Secretary on 4 February, 1959:

> To consider and recommend to the Governor the form of direct elections on a common roll for the representative members of the Legislative Council to be introduced in 1961, the number of representative seats to be filled under the above system, their allocation among different areas of the Protectorate and the method of ensuring that there will be adequate representation on the Legislative Council for non-Africans [27].

Also stated, but not within the terms of reference, was the provision that the Committee might be required to advise on issues that were related to its terms of reference, such as the size and composition of the Ugandan Legislature and possibly the form of government. It was emphasized, however, that "these are matters on which a very special responsibility lies directly with Her Majesty's Government and cannot be settled here in Uganda". The committee therefore was merely required to provide advice on those matters.

After a year of detailed country- wide discussion, except in Buganda where the local government refused to co-operate, the Committee's report was presented to the Governor in December 1959.

Among the recommendations made in this report were: (i) that "direct elections should be held in all parts of the country on the next occasion", and that "no option should be offered to the alternative of indirect elections" [28]; (ii) that elections should be held as soon as possible, and certainly not latter than 1961, and that adult suffrage should be the qualification for voting [29]; (iii) that a common roll should be introduced, but that the inclusion on the roll should not establish any claim to citizenship or any rights to the land [30]; (iv) that the number of representatives on the Legislative Council should be increased to eighty and be distributed as follows: 20 for Buganda, 22 for eastern Province, 18 for western

Province, 15 for northern Province, and 5 for urban areas [31]; and (v) that non-Africans should be included on the common roll and be represented like everybody else in Uganda, and that any other attempts to safeguard the position of non-Africans in the country might in the long run do more harm than good.

The report also provided advice where it was required to do so: (i) that the next Legislative Council should be called the National Assembly, with a cabinet that should be responsible to the Legislature; (ii) that apart from the Chief Secretary, the Attorney-General, and the Minister of Finance, the National Assembly should be composed of directly elected representatives, and that the party with a majority in the Assembly should be invited to form the government, composed of a Chief Minister and a Council of Ministers;(iii) that the Council of Ministers should be responsible to the National Assembly and not to the Governor, although the latter should continue to have reserved powers to veto the decisions of the former, should it be necessary to do so; and (iv) that after the next elections, a conference should be held to consider the form of government that was suitable for Uganda, and that this conference should be attended not only by official representatives of local governments, but also by representatives elected by each local government specifically for this conference [32].

With some minor modifications, the report of the Constitutional Committee was accepted by both the Governor and the Secretary of State for Colonies [33]. However, the Buganda government totally rejected the report, arguing that the terms of reference under which the Committee was constituted included a consideration of special representation for non-Africans on the Legislative Council.

The Relationships Commission

At least two factors led to the appointment of this Commission. First, as mentioned above, the Constitutional Committee had recommended that a conference should be held to consider a type of government that was suitable for an independent Uganda. The Relationship Commission was appointed in place of this conference. And second, since Buganda had rejected the report of the Constitutional Committee and threatened to secede from the rest of Uganda, the Commission was appointed to ensure that Buganda was to remain part of an independent Uganda. The Relationships Commission was appointed in 1960 with the following terms of reference:

> To consider the future form of government best suited for Uganda and the question of relationship between the central Government and other authorities in Uganda bearing in mind, (a) Her Majesty's Governments'

known resolve to lead Uganda by appropriate stages to independence and to this end to develop stable institutions of government which will properly reflect the particular circumstances and needs of Uganda; and (b) the desire of the people of Uganda to preserve their existing institutions and customs and the status and dignity of their rulers and leaders; and (c) the special relationship that already exists between Her Majesty's Government and His Highness the Kabaka's government and the native governments of Bunyoro, Ankole and Toro as set down in various Agreements that have been made with traditional rulers and people of Buganda, Bunyoro, Ankole, and Toro, and to make recommendations [34].

When the Commission reported in   June 1961, it made the following recommendations: (i) that while Uganda should remain a single democratic state with a strong central government, the relationship between that government and the kingdom of Buganda should be federal in nature, primarily because Buganda already enjoyed a federal status and, thus, it would be unrealistic to expect Buganda to accept a new constitution with less autonomy than it already enjoyed [35]; (ii) that the central government should have powers over foreign affairs, nationality of Uganda, the armed forces, and the police, and that the kingdom of Buganda should have exclusive powers over the Kabakaship, the Lukiiko, and all its traditional institutions; (iii) that the residual power should be shared between Buganda and the central government, subject to the

70

latter's overriding power in the last resort, and that the ultimate court of appeal for these constitutional matters should be the Privy Council in London to ensure complete impartiality [36]; (iv) that the relationship between the kingdoms of western Uganda and the central government should be semi-federal, since the former lacked autonomy that was comparable to that of Buganda [37]; (v) that the other local governments in the country should be under a unitary system, partly because they were a "recent creation" and partly because they had overwhelmingly indicated a strong preference for unitarism over federalism in their choice of the form of government for Uganda [38]; and (vi) that no local government in the country, with the exception of Buganda, should be allowed to opt for indirect elections for their representatives to the national Parliament [39].

Thus, the Relationships Commission supported constitutionally entrenched power inequalities among the ethnic-centered local governments which, as was indicated in the last chapter, had been created by the colonial state.

Another constitutional problem which was considered by the Relationships Commission, and which is relevant in this study, was the boundary dispute between Buganda and Bunyoro. Realizing the seriousness of problems that this dispute was likely to cause in

71

Uganda, the Commission recommended that a referendum should be held in the two counties of Buyaga and Bugangazi before Uganda's independence to determine whether the people living in the area wished to remain under the administration of Buganda or to join Bunyoro.

In the remaining part of this chapter I will analyze the extent to which the recommendations of this commission influenced the formulation of the subsequent Independence Constitution.

The First Constitutional Conference

The purpose of this conference was to discuss the recommendations of the Relationships Commission, and to decide whether to adopt them as the constitution for Uganda's self-government. The conference was attended by delegates from all local governments in Uganda, and representatives of the two leading political parties in the country at the time, the UPC and the DP.

The conference opened at Lancaster House in London on September 18, 1961, under the Chairmanship of the Right Hon. Ian Macleod, the Secretary of State for the Colonies. In his opening speech, the Secretary of State announced that within two years Uganda was to assume full responsibility over its affairs and that, in his opinion, the Relationships Commission had provided a framework within which the conference could reach agreement on a constitution that was to take Uganda to the stage of self-government [40].

Although the recommendations made by the Relationships Commission were discussed and adopted by the conference one by one, two of them caused considerable disagreements among delegates. The first major disagreement was over Buganda's constitutional right to opt for an indirect method of electing its representatives to the national Parliament. Benedicto Kiwanuka, the President of the DP and Chief Minister of the Ugandan government at the time, protested strongly against this recommendation. Kiwanuka argued that in accordance with the Buganda Agreement of 1955, Buganda was to elect its representatives to Parliament through a direct method, and that this provision was being breached without any reason being given for doing so. He argued further that indirect elections were inherently anti-democratic and dangerous to party politics, since the indirectly elected members might decide to side with a minority party in

Parliament, undermining thereby the decision of the national electorate [41].

To the surprise of some observers, Milton Obote, the President of the UPC, supported the recommendation, arguing as follows:

> I think that the proposals were formulated in the light of the prevailing situation in Buganda. It was vital that the people of Buganda should recognize the central government. In my view it was better that this be achieved through indirect elections than that the existing situation be allowed to continue [42].

Despite the threat by the DP delegates to walk out of the conference if this recommendation was adopted, it was passed and embodied in Uganda's self-government constitution.

The second major disagreement was over the dispute between Buganda and Bunyoro. Buganda's delegates were adamantly opposed to the recommendation that a referendum should be held in the disputed area. The delegates from Bunyoro, for their part, insisted that since the lost counties problem was created by the British, it was incumbent on them to settle the dispute before Uganda's independence. The Secretary of State then promised that he would request the British Government to appoint a

74

commission of Privy Councilors to study and provide a comprehensive report on the dispute. The rest of the recommendations made by the Relationships Commission were incorporated in a draft for the constitution of Uganda's self-government.

The final draft provided the Governor with power over foreign affairs, the armed forces, and the police [43]. The rest of the powers of the central government of Uganda were to be in the hands of the Council of Ministers responsible to the National Assembly [44]. It was also agreed that Uganda would achieve internal government on March 1, 1962, and that pre-independence elections would be held in April 1962.

The Second Constitutional Conference

The second constitutional conference was also held in London, and was attended by delegates representing the same political groups as previously [45]. The major objective of this conference was to resolve the remaining constitutional problems, and to prepare the Independence Constitution for Uganda. Three major problems were confronted at this conference: (i) the demand for a federal status by the kingdoms of western Uganda; (ii) the demand for more power by the kingdom of Buganda; and (iii) the dispute between Buganda and Bunyoro over the lost counties.

The kingdoms of western Uganda were not satisfied with the semi-federal status that they had been accorded. The sources of their dissatisfaction were: (i) that this status was inferior to that of Buganda, and (ii) that a new Agreement had been signed between the British Crown and Buganda on 31 October, 1961, but not with them. Consequently, prior to the second constitutional conference the rulers of these kingdoms went to London to present their grievances to the Secretary of State for the Colonies. With these rulers also went the ruler of the district of Busoga (the Kyabazinga), who demanded a federal status for Busoga and an opportunity to sign an agreement with the British Crown. During the June conference, therefore, delegates from Busoga and the three kingdoms of western Uganda were fighting for an equal status with Buganda. Grace Ibingira, himself a delegate of the UPC/KY coalition government at this conference, has summarized the wishes of these rulers as follows:

> The attitudes of these kingdoms during the conference detracted from its progress. They wished to conclude Agreements with the British government regardless of how short-lived they would be. The Omukama

(king) of Toro, supporting the attitude of his delegation, confirmed he would prefer to have Toro's Agreement successfully concluded even if it meant postponing the date of Uganda's independence [46].

For their own satisfaction, the kingdoms of western Uganda were allowed to conclude Agreements with the British government, which however, were to terminate on Uganda's independence only four months ahead. It was also agreed that these kingdoms were to be called "federal states", although this title was not to be accompanied by the possession of exclusive powers similar to those of Buganda. In fact it was even made clear that this title was not to apply to Buganda, indicating thereby that these kingdoms were to remain inferior to Buganda despite their new title. The District of Busoga was denied an opportunity to sign an Agreement with the British government, but was granted the title of "territory" which, for unknown reasons, was strongly demanded by Busoga's delegates in the conference.

For its part, the kingdom of Buganda demanded more power during this second constitutional conference. Buganda's delegates demanded that the Kabaka's government should always be consulted whenever the national Parliament discussed bills dealing with: immigration, passports, defense, and internal security. This demand was rejected on the ground that these issues were the sole

77

responsibility of the central government of Uganda. Buganda delegates then demanded that the Kabaka's government should be given power to appoint and dismiss Judges of the High Court of Buganda. When this demand was rejected, on the ground that the Uganda Judicial Service Commission was to retain these powers, Buganda delegates tenaciously demanded that the Kabaka's government should have the power to establish, maintain, and control its own police force [47]. After a lengthy debate, it was agreed that the Kabaka would have a police force, but that its discipline was to be the responsibility of the Buganda Public Service, in consultation with the Uganda Inspector General of Police.

Finally, the conference was required to resolve the half-century dispute between Buganda and Bunyoro over the lost counties. A Commission of Privy Councilors, under the Chairmanship of Lord Molson, had studied the dispute and recommended that the two counties of Buyaga and Buganganzi should be transferred from Buganda to Bunyoro before Uganda's independence [48].

Buganda delegates refused to accept this recommendation, and the Secretary of State announced that he had himself made the final decisions relating to the dispute: (i) that the administration of these counties was to be taken over by the central government of Uganda; and (ii) that within at least two years after Uganda's independence, a referendum should be held in the area to provide the inhabitants with the opportunity to decide whether they wished to stay in Buganda or to be transferred back to Bunyoro.

Prime Minister Milton Obote accepted the central government's responsibility to administer the disputed area, despite the lack of agreement between Buganda and Bunyoro over the above-mentioned decisions.

Other matters that were considered by the June conference dealt mainly with fiscal arrangements, based on the recommendations of the Fiscal Commission that had visited Uganda in early 1962 [49]. Otherwise, most of what was contained in the self-government constitution was adopted in the Independence Constitution, which was laid before the Uganda Parliament on 2 October, 1962, as the Uganda (Independence) Order-in-Council, 1962.

On 9 October, 1962, the Duke of Kent, representing the Queen of England, handed over the instruments of power to Prime Minister Obote, marking thereby the political independence of Uganda.

CONCLUSION

On the basis of the preceding discussion at least four major constraints, both real and potential, on political order in Uganda can be identified. First, instead of neutralizing cultural cleavages as a measure to promote political accommodation among sub-national groups in the country, political parties that developed in Uganda made these cleavages the cornerstones of their organization. Both the DP and the UPC were developed along religious lines: Catholicism and Protestantism, respectively. On the other hand, the KY was developed on an ethnic foundation, being purely a Baganda party. Second, far from redressing pre-existing power inequalities among the ethnic-centered local governments in Uganda, the Independence Constitution provided them with legal recognition, thereby promoting potential constitutional conflicts among sub-national groups in the country. Third, the Independence Constitution left unresolved the half-century conflict between Buganda and Bunyoro over the lost counties, a problem that had every potential to create political instability in an independent Uganda. And, finally, having been denied an early opportunity to interact politically at the national level, and having failed to develop a nationalist movement on the basis of which a measure of political accommodation could be promoted among

80

sub-national groups in the country, Ugandan political elites were mainly concerned with the acquisition of political power as an end in itself.

The political alliance between the UPC and the KY, whose respective leaders had widely divergent views on almost every conceivable policy, was a candid demonstration of an unambiguous desire on the part of the political elites involved to acquire and exercise political power, regardless of what the consequences might be.

In the next chapter an attempt will be made to examine the extent to which the immediate post-colonial government under the leadership of Prime Minister Obote, dealt with the above and other related constraints on political order in Uganda.

NOTES

[1] Both political parties and constitutions, whose development involved active participation of the colonized peoples, were expected at least to promote accommodation among sub-national groups within their respective colonies. See J.M. Lee, Colonial Development and Good Government: A Study of Ideas Expressed by the British Official Classes in Planning Decolonization 1939-1964 London, Oxford University Press, 1967, pp.172-188.

[2] See especially the introduction and conclusion in James Coleman and Carl Rosberg (eds.), Political Parties and National Integration in Tropical Africa, Berkeley, University of California Press, 1966; R. Emerson, "Parties and National Integration in Africa", in M. Weiner and J. LaPalombara (eds.), Political Parties and Political Development, Princeton, Princeton University Press, 1966, pp.267-302; and David Apter, The Politics of Modernization, Chicago, University of Chicago Press, 1967, pp.313-356.

[3] See especially, Arnold Rivkin (ed), Nations by Design: Institution-Building in Africa, New York, Doubleday Company, 1968, pp.1-34; and Gerald Heeger, The Politics of Underdevelopment, New York, St. Martin's Press, 1974, pp.45-51.

[4] Myron Weiner, Party-Building in a New Nation: The Indian National Congress, Chicago, University of Chicago Press, 1967, introduction.

[5] Anthony Low, Buganda in Modern History, London, Weidenfield and Nicolson, 1971, p.202. The argument here is that the reforms carried out during the post-second World War, especially by Governor Andrew Cohen, made it clear to the Ugandan political elites that their country was being prepared for self-government which, in turn, reduced the urge for these elites to develop a nationalist movement whose purpose in other colonies was mainly to fight for political independence.

[6] See especially Anthony Low, Political Parties in Uganda 1949-1962, London, Athlone Press, 1962, pp.7-43; and Cranford Pratt, "Nationalism in Uganda", Political Studies, 9 (1961) pp.157-178.

[7] Musazi, who founded the UNC in 1952, had been imprisoned for one and a half years on the charge that he forged names on a petition against compulsory recruitment of Ugandans into the King's Rifles for the purpose of fighting in the Second World War on behalf of Britain. In 1945, he was deported from Buganda for his involvement in the riots that took place in Buganda that year. When

he returned from exile, Musazi founded the Uganda African Farmers Union (UAFU) which, however, was proscribed by the government for its involvement in the riots which occurred in Buganda in 1949. In the wake of these frustrations, Musazi decided to form a national party, the UNC, in 1952.

[8] For a detailed discussion on the UNC, see David Apter, The Political Kingdom in Uganda: A Study in Bureaucratic Nationalism, Princeton, Princeton University Press, 1961, pp,310-336.

[9] See Francis Morris and James Read, Uganda: The Development of Its Laws and Constitution, London, Stevens and Sons, 1966, pp.63-65.

[10] As discussed in chapter two, the colonial power politicised religion by providing more favors to Protestants than any other denomination in the country. This so-called Protestant establishment provoked resentment among Catholics who were numerically stronger than Protestants both in Buganda and the country as a whole. For a discussion on the impact of religion on the Ugandan politics, see especially: F.B. Welbourn, Religion and Politics in Uganda, 1952-1962, Nairobi, East African Publishing

House, 1965; and K.G. Lockard, "Religion and Politics in Independent Uganda: Movement Toward Secularization", in James Scarritt (ed), Analysing Political Change in Africa: Application of a New Multidimensional Framework, Boulder, Westview, 1980, pp.40-73.

[11] See James Mulira, "Nationalism and Communist Phobia in Colonial Uganda", Mawazo, 5 (June 1983) pp.3-16.

[12] See Kenneth Ingham, The Making of Modern Uganda, London, George Allen and Unwin, 1958, pp.51-53.

[13] Welbourn, Religion and Politics in Uganda, pp.17-18.

[14] Ibid, p.17.

[15] See Forward to Freedom, the DP Manifesto, Kampala, Patel Press,1960, p. 1.

[16] For an account of these elections throughout Uganda, see Welbourn, Religion and Politics in Uganda, pp. 21-24.

[17] Ibid, p.25.

[18] For a discussion on the development and impact of Kabaka Yekka on Ugandan politics, see especially: Ian Hancock, "Patriotism and neo-Traditionalism in Buganda: The Kabaka Yekka (The King Alone) Movement 1961-1962", Journal of African History, 11(1970) pp.419-434; C. Gertzel, "How Kabaka Yekka Came To Be", African Report, 9(October 1964) pp.9-13; and Nelson Kasfir, The Shrinking Political Arena: Participation and Ethnicity in African Politics, With a Case Study of Uganda, Berkeley, University of California Press, 1976, pp.119-126.

[19] Welbourn, Religion and Politics in Uganda, pp. 30-41. Unfortunately, Kiwanuka himself could not make it to Parliament and Basil Bataringaya became the leader of the DP in Parliament while Kiwanuka remained the national President of the party.

[20] See Grace Ibingira, The Forging of an African Nation: The Political and Constitutional Evolution of Uganda from Colonial Rule to Independence, 1894-1962, New York, The Viking Press, 1973, p.87.

[21] See Report of the Constitutional Committee, 1959, Entebbe, Government Printer, 1959.

[22] See Akiiki Mujaju, "The Role of UPC as a Party of Government in Uganda", Canadian Journal of African Studies, 10(1976) pp.443-467.

[23] This problem was common to the DP as well. In the Parliamentary elections of 1962, only one MP was elected outside his place of birth. See Nelson Kasfir, "Cultural Sub-nationalism in Uganda", in Victor Olorunsola (ed), The Politics of Cultural Sub-nationalism, New York, Doubleday, 1972, pp.51-148, at p.86.

[24] See Thomas Hopkins, "Politics in Uganda: The Buganda Question", in J. Butler and A.A. Castgno (eds.), Boston University Papers on Africa, New York, Praeger, 1967, pp.251-290.

[25] Edward McWhinney, Constitution Making Principles, Process, Practice, Toronto, University of Toronto Press, 1981, pp.3-23.

[26] See Ibingira, The Forging of an African Nation, pp.1-16.

[27] See Uganda Protectorate, Proceedings of the Legislative Council, 1958/59, Part I, p.95.

[28] See Uganda Protectorate, Report of the Constitutional Committee 1959, paragraphs 41-42.

[29] Ibid. paragraphs 93-95.

[30] Ibid. paragraphs 51-52.

[31] Ibid., paragraph 66.

[32] Ibid., paragraphs 151-152.

[33] The modification was that the Council of Ministers should be advisory to, and be advised by, the Governor since most of its members might still lack experience on legislative and constitutional matters.

[34] Uganda Protectorate, Report of the Uganda Relationships Commission, Entebbe, Government Printer, 1961. The Chairman of the Commission was the Right Hon. Earl of Munster, P.C., K.B.E. It is important to note that the recommendation of the Constitutional Committee that a conference composed of representatives from all local governments in Uganda should be established to consider the form of government that was suitable for Uganda, was overlooked

by the Colonial Office which, instead, appointed the Relationships Commission to determine the future form of government for Uganda.

[35] Ibid., paragraphs 99-105.

[36] Ibid., paragraphs 123-124.

[37] Ibid., paragraph 128.

[38] Ibid., paragraphs 142-146.

[39] Ibid., paragraphs 151-154.

[40] Uganda Protectorate, Report of Uganda Constitutional Conference, Entebbe, Government Printer, 1961.

[41] Ibid., p.5

[42] Ibid., p.7. Obote's support for Buganda's constitutional demands was intended, in turn, to win the support of Buganda, without which his political party could not lead Uganda to independence. What surprised some observers of Ugandan politics

at the time, however, was that the same Milton Obote had strongly opposed the method of indirect elections to Parliament two years earlier when he was a member of the constitutional committee in 1959.

[43] Uganda Protectorate, Uganda Internal Self Government Constitution, Entebbe, Government Printer, 1962, Section 60.

[44] Ibid., Sections 53-54.

[45] During the pre-independence elections in Uganda, which were held two months prior to this conference, the DP lost all its seats in Buganda and won only 24 seats in the rest of Uganda. The UPC won 37 seats and the KY 21 seats, which were indirectly elected by the Buganda Lukiiko. In accordance with pre-election agreement, the UPC and the KY formed a coalition government, headed by Milton Obote who chose his cabinet from both parties. During this second constitutional conference, therefore, the DP was no longer the party of government.

[46] Ibingira, The Forging of an African Nation, p.276.

[47] Ibid.

[48] Uganda Protectorate, <u>Report of the Commission of Privy Councillors on a Dispute Between Buganda and Bunyoro</u>, Entebbe, Government Printer, May 1962.

[49] Uganda Protectorate, <u>Report of the Uganda Fiscal Commission,</u>
Entebbe, Government Printer, 1962.

CONSTRAINTS ON POLITICAL ORDER IN UGANDA

CHAPTER IV

MILTON OBOTE'S FIRST REGIME (1962-1971)

The literature on the post-colonial state in Africa has emphasized at least four sources of constraints on political order, arising mainly from the quality of leadership: (i) the failure of political leaders to acquire popular legitimacy [1], leading them to pursue personal, rather than institutionalized rule [2]; (ii) the tendency of these leaders to foster sectional identifications as a means of securing access to political power and to scarce economic resources [3]; (iii) the failure of the leadership to establish effective control over the military [4]; and (iv) the leadership's mismanagement of the economy [5].

All these sources of constraints are valid. But what is less emphasized in the literature is the fact that post-colonial leaders in Africa have themselves been confronted with some constraints, arising mainly from the colonial legacy and the political environment within which they have operated [6].

It appears appropriate, therefore, first to examine constraints inherited by African leaders at independence before discussing those constraints arising from their leadership, since explanations for some of the latter may well lie in the former.

The main concerns of this chapter, therefore, are first, to discuss the impact of the colonial legacy on Obote's leadership (1962-1971) and, second, to examine the extent to which Obote's leadership during this period enhanced or contained the above-mentioned constraints on political order in Uganda.

The Impact of the Colonial Legacy

As indicated in preceding chapters, a number of constraints on political order in Uganda developed mainly during the colonial period, and some of these persisted into the post-independence era. In particular, issues which dominated Ugandan politics during the first half of Obote's leadership (1962-1967) involved: Buganda's relationship to the centre, the dispute between Buganda and Bunyoro over the lost counties, and inter-elite conflicts arising from the previous colonial politicization of cultural cleavages.

In order to secure Uganda's smooth transition to political independence under his leadership, Milton Obote decided to flow with the historical current of Uganda at the time by recognizing the pre-eminence of Buganda within Uganda, which had been nurtured throughout the colonial period.

First, during the pre-independence constitutional negotiations in London, Obote supported the most important of Buganda's demands, including a full federal relationship with the central government, and the right to opt for an indirect method of electing Buganda's representatives to the national Parliament. Second, a political alliance between Obote's UPC and the Buganda-based KY was signed by both Obote and the Kabaka of Buganda with the intention of removing the DP from power and, subsequently, forming a coalition government that would lead Uganda to political independence. Finally, as part of this alliance, the UPC/KY coalition government headed by Prime Minister Obote elected the Kabaka of Buganda, Sir Edward Mutesa II, to the newly created position of ceremonial President a year after Uganda's independence.

However, the UPC/KY alliance, on the basis of which Buganda was integrated into the central government of Uganda, was quickly put under strain during the early years of independence. First, contrary to the terms of the alliance, the UPC began to establish political party branches within Buganda as early as 1963 [7].

Second, the vague constitutional provisions on the basis of which the central government was to finance social services in Buganda, which the latter had interpreted to mean receiving an unlimited flow of finance from the centre, were resolved in favor of the central government by the High Court of Uganda in 1964.

Third, when a referendum was held in the lost counties of Buyaga and Bugangazi in November 1964, against strong opposition from Buganda, the overwhelming majority of inhabitants voted in favor of a return to Bunyoro [8], leading to Buganda's loss of a territory that it had acquired, albeit by default, at the beginning of colonial rule in Uganda.

And finally, during the period 1964-65 some MPs from the DP and the KY defected into the UPC, enabling the latter to attain a clear majority in Parliament on the strength of which Prime Minister Obote decided to terminate the UPC/KY alliance, thereby ending the coalition government in Uganda [9].

Although these actions helped Obote to consolidate power at the centre, they also exacerbated tensions between the Baganda and Obote's central government, leading the former to seek means of ousting Obote from leadership.

In the course of 1965, two hostile political camps developed within the central government of Uganda: the one headed by Edward Mutesa and Grace Ibingira which drew most of its support, both within and outside the Parliament, from southern Uganda; and the other headed by Milton Obote and Felix Onama which drew its support mainly from northern Uganda.

As will be indicated below, this inter-elite conflict culminated in the Ugandan Constitutional crisis of 1966 during which Prime Minister Obote, with the help of the northern-dominated Ugandan Army, subdued his opponents.

In February 1966 Daudi Ochieng, a popular spokesman of the KY, introduced a motion in the national Parliament calling for a Commission of Inquiry into his allegations that Colonel Idi Amin, then Deputy Commander of the Uganda Army, had smuggled gold and ivory from the Congo, and had shared profits with Prime Minister Obote and two of his closest Cabinet colleagues. The motion was accepted by the majority of MPs present, including some of Obote's cabinet Ministers [10].

On his return from a tour in northern Uganda, Obote acted swiftly to counter this move. Having secured the support of the military,

Obote called a cabinet meeting at which he ordered the arrest of five ministers, all from southern Uganda and believed to have been sympathetic to Buganda [11].

The Prime Minister then disclosed that Edward Mutesa, in his capacity as the President, had sought military help from the British High Commission in Uganda in the event that the Uganda Army should attempt to overthrow the independence constitution. This Mutesa admitted [12], and Obote dismissed him as President. Obote then suspended the independence constitution and assumed all executive powers in the country.

Following his announcement of the composition of the Commission of Inquiry to investigate the allegations against Colonel Amin [13], Prime Minister Obote called an emergency session of Parliament in which he introduced an interim constitution to replace the Independence Constitution [14]. Among the radical changes introduced by this interim constitution were: the abolition of all elements of federalism in Uganda; the replacement of the position of the ceremonial President by an executive one, a position that was assumed by Obote himself; the abolition of Buganda's constitutional right to opt for an indirect method of electing its representatives to the national Parliament; and the provision that all public officers, including officials of local government, were to be appointed by the central government.

In reaction to these changes, which essentially eradicated the existing special status of Buganda, the government of Buganda passed a resolution asking Obote's central government to withdraw its offices from Buganda soil within ten days. Obote regarded this order from Buganda as an act of treason and on 24 May, 1966, he sent the Uganda Army to take over the Kabaka's palace. The Kabaka and his prime minister fled into exile in England where the former died in 1969 [15].

The Republican Constitution which was adopted by Parliament in 1967 retained all the radical reforms that had been introduced by the interim constitution of 1966, and added more radical changes, including: the abolition of kingdoms altogether [16]; the division of Buganda into four districts, each of which was to be administered by a District Commissioner appointed by the central government, like any other district in the country [17]; and the centralization of power, especially in the institution of the Presidency [18].

At least three conclusions can be drawn thus far. First, the Ugandan constitutional crisis of 1966 was prompted mainly by constraints inherited at independence. Second, through this crisis, Buganda's anomalous position of a state within a state was ultimately brought to an end. And finally, by involving the military in Ugandan politics, first to abrogate the Independence Constitution and, second, to subdue his political opponents, Prime Minister Obote "encouraged the soldiers to cast their eyes on the ultimate seat of power" [19]. In the remaining part of this chapter I will discuss Obote's leadership (1962-1971) in relation to other factors mentioned at the beginning of this chapter.

Obote's Lack of Popular Legitimacy

In theory, political leaders may acquire legitimate authority in three main ways [20]. First, on **rational grounds**, where leaders are elected to political offices which themselves have acquired such a strong legitimacy as to sustain most occupants (legal authority). Here obedience is owed to the legally established impersonal political institutions which leaders occupy. Second, on **traditional grounds,** where leaders' legitimacy derives from established beliefs in the sanctity of immemorial traditions on the basis of which such leaders exercise authority (traditional authority). Here obedience is owed to the person of the chief who occupies the traditionally sanctioned position of authority and who is bound by such tradition. And finally, on **charismatic grounds**, where leaders may acquire legitimacy on the basis of their exceptional personal qualities which enable them to win support of the governed (charismatic authority). Here a leader is obeyed by virtue of personal trust, which the governed have towards the leader's exceptional qualities.

Lacking long established political institutions with a capacity to win both the support and the faith of the governed, African leaders can hardly rely on legal or institutional legitimacy. Instead, some of these leaders have been more inclined to uproot the existing political institutions, especially when their own interests are at stake, than to conform to institutional procedures. Obote's abrogation of the Ugandan Independence Constitution in 1966 is a case in point.

On the other hand, popular legitimacy based on charismatic leadership requires that the leader in question enjoys the support of charismatic norms [21]. According to Max Weber, charismatic norms include:

> quality of an individual personality by virtue of which he is set apart from ordinary men and treated as endowed with supernatural, superhuman, or at least specifically exceptional powers or qualities. These are such as

are not accessible to the ordinary person, but are regarded as of divine origin or as exemplary, and on the basis of them the individual is treated as a leader [22].

Obote's personality seems to have been the antithesis of charismatic norms as given above by Weber. "The remarkable thing about Obote," writes Uzoigwe, "was his lack of obvious attributes that would elevate him above his peers" [23]. Among other factors, at least two worked against Obote's acquiring popular legitimacy on the basis of charismatic qualities. First, Obote came from northern Uganda, which remained underdeveloped during the colonial period and was, therefore, regarded as "backward" by people from southern Uganda who had enjoyed a measure of socio-economic and political growth during the colonial era. And second, Obote's limited education was scorned by Ugandan intellectuals.

Moreover, coming from a non-monarchical Langi ethnic group in northern Uganda, Obote's humble background was disdained by traditional kings of southern Uganda over whom he exercised authority. Thus failing to acquire popular legitimacy on any of the above-mentioned bases of authority, Obote relied on his ingenuity to keep himself in power. According to Mazrui,

102

Faced with a very difficult country, coming from a tribe which had not been specifically privileged during the colonial period, battling against a Ganda supremacy which could not be overthrown overnight, bereft of a Martyrdom in his personal biography, lacking warm public personality, Milton Obote had to rely on his ability to understand the intricacies of tactical and strategic political calculations [24].

Obote's leadership traits, as portrayed by Mazrui, turned him ultimately into a personal ruler. In the next section an attempt will be made to analyze the extent to which Obote practiced personal rule during his first leadership (1962-1971).

Obote as a Personal Ruler

In theory, personal rule entails, among other things, three main characteristics: the leader's excessive reliance on personal loyalty; the use of coercion to enforce public compliance; and an extensive application of patron-client linkages as a means to sustain the leader in power [25]. I will now examine some factors that led Obote to rely on personal rule.

Milton Obote occupied an unenviable weak position when he became the Prime Minister of Uganda at independence in 1962. His political party, the UPC, was not sufficiently strong to lead Uganda to political independence and, as mentioned above, Obote

103

had to forge a coalition with the Buganda-based KY party in order to acquire additional Parliamentary support.

Meanwhile, the economically and educationally disadvantaged northerners, including Obote himself, feared domination by southerners who already occupied top echelons of the Ugandan civil service.

However, the colonial administration had unwittingly created a situation, which Obote could manipulate to his advantage. The Uganda Army that Obote's leadership inherited at independence had been recruited largely from among northerners, whom the colonial government had considered to be reliable soldiers and to exhibit physical martial qualities.

In his search for personal loyalty, Obote and his lieutenants seized the opportunity to use the army as a power base. Having appointed a fellow-northerner, Felix Onama, as the Minister of Defense and initiated the rapid expansion of the Uganda Army (from about 1,000 armed forces at independence in 1962 to about 6,000 in 1967), he recruited a disproportionate number of soldiers from the north, with the intention of ensuring continued northern dominance in the army [26].

Obote manipulated yet another situation to his advantage. Following army mutinies in Uganda, Kenya, and Tanganyika (now mainland Tanzania) in January 1964, there were radical reforms in the army in the latter two East African states but none in Uganda [27]. In Kenya, mutineers were dismissed from the army and their leaders were detained. Thereafter the Kenyan army was reconstructed, with the help of British army officers, along the lines of a professional military bureaucracy. In Tanganyika, mutineers were dismissed and the army was integrated more closely with the ruling political party (TANU), and a Para-military national service was established as a balancing force to the regular army [28]. In Uganda, no real reconstruction took place. Instead, the demands made by mutineers were met by Obote's government [29]. As well, some of the mutineers who originally had been dismissed from the army were later recalled to service [30].

As some analysts have suggested [31], Obote seems to have taken advantage of the army mutiny in Uganda to further his search for personal loyalty. For, in the wake of this mutiny, Obote announced a number of promotions within the army without consulting President Mutesa, as he was required to do by the constitution [32].

105

Among these promotions, one turned out to be particularly vital to Obote's search for personal loyalty. Contrary to the advice of the departing colonial officials that Idi Amin should be retired from the Uganda Army, following charges brought against him of using great brutality against the Turkana ethnic group at the Uganda/Kenya border in 1961 [33], Milton Obote promoted Idi Amin to the position of the Deputy Commander of the Uganda Army.

Within two years after this promotion, Amin was again under attack, but this time from the Ugandan Parliament which demanded his suspension pending an investigation into an allegation that he had been involved in smuggling gold and ivory from the neighboring Congo. Obote's response to this parliamentary demand was to send Amin on leave and, soon afterwards, to promote him to the top position of Army Commander.

The grooming of Amin by Obote was mainly inspired by the latter's involvement in the struggle for power based on the south-north axis. Since the southern camp had won the support of the Army Commander -- Brigadier Shaban Opolot -- the northern camp headed by Obote decided to peg its trust on Amin who, after all, was a fellow northerner. Having jailed Opolot in early 1966, on the ground that he was involved in a plot, together with Mutesa and

Ibingira, to overthrow the government [34], Obote promoted Amin to the position of the Army Commander.

Obote's search for the loyalty of the Uganda Army had its pay-offs, albeit only in the short-run. With the support of the army, Milton Obote abrogated the Independence Constitution early in 1966; and by the middle of the following year the army had helped him to transform the Ugandan political system from a quasi-federal to a unitary state, with centralized powers in his hands as executive President of the Ugandan republic. During this constitutional crisis and after, Obote's political enemies; and more particularly the Baganda, were treated by the Uganda Army as conquered people. This was reflected, among other things, in the indefinite state of emergency that was declared over Buganda from 1966 up to the fall of Obote's first regime in 1971.

Sectionalism Leading to Intra-Elite Conflict

As indicated in chapter one, sectionalism entails competition and conflict between leaders of subgroups over access to political power, wealth and status. Apart from the inter-elite conflict that led to the constitutional crisis of 1966, Obote's first term of office (1962-1971) was also characterized by intra-elite conflict. This type of conflict, which entails a clear split within the leadership of a political

107

subgroup whose members have shared a common political alignment in the past, occurred between President Obote and his army Commander - General Idi Amin -- leading to the seizure of power by the latter in January 1971.

Despite their joint efforts to subdue their political opponents from southern Uganda during most of the 1960s, the politically dominant elites from northern Uganda began to conflict with each other during the late 1960s and the early 1970s, the main protagonists being President Obote and his army commander, Idi Amin.

On 19 December 1969, there was an attempt on Obote's life. Hardly a month later the Second-in-Command of the Uganda Army and a favorite of Obote's, Brigadier Okoya, along with his wife were murdered at their home in Gulu. Okoya's death cast suspicion on Amin for at least three reasons: (i) there was high probability of Obote promoting Okoya to replace Amin, since the former was more educated, better trained militarily, and, being an Acholi, ethnically closer to Obote; (ii) Okoya had all along been critical of Amin's tendency to favor the non-commissioned officers from his home district of West Nile; and (iii) Okoya is alleged to have accused Amin of cowardice, for having fled the scene immediately after the attempted assassination on the President. And it was also rumored that Okoya was gradually uncovering Amin's participation in a plot that led to this attempted assassination [35].

In his attempt to neutralize the army, Obote shifted resources to two other branches of the security forces which were more loyal to him:(i) the General Service Unit, an intelligence service that operated from the President's Office under the command of Obote's cousin, Akena Adoko; and (ii) the Special Force, which was a paramilitary branch of the police.

In addition, when Obote sent Amin to represent Uganda at the funeral of President Nasser of Egypt, he appointed a new army chief of staff and a new commanding officer for the Air Force. He also announced other promotions in security forces during this short period when the Army Commander was away. In September 1970, Obote carried out another massive reorganization in the army that placed his supporters, mainly from Lango and Acholi, in twenty key military posts [36].

Thus, shunted-away from sole supreme command of the army, Amin sought to outmaneuver his boss and former political ally. On the advice of Israeli Military Officers [37], who at the time were in Uganda on a training mission, Amin transferred troops and officers personally loyal to him, mainly his West Nile and Nubian allies, to command posts in the strategic Malire Regiment on the outskirts of Kampala and armed them with the strongest weapons available [38]. When the showdown ultimately came in January 1971, the Malire Regiment executed a successful coup and Obote went into exile in Tanzania.

Subjective Control over the Military

On the basis of the foregoing discussion it should be clear that the type of control that Obote exercised over his military was subjective rather than objective [39]. Obote's failure to develop the Ugandan Army along the lines of military professionalism was based primarily on his desire to utilize security forces for his own political survival. In particular, his involvement of the military in the management of domestic political crises in the middle of 1960s brought the army closer to the threshold of direct political intervention, for, as Uzoigwe has rightly argued, "the responsibility for politicizing the military must be placed squarely on Obote's shoulders because in his struggle for survival he helped to nurse their political ambitions" [40].

Moreover, far from developing an ethnically balanced military for the purpose, among other things, of improving a broad relationship between the army and the larger Ugandan society, Obote's military policy was biased in both recruitment and promotions in favor, first, of the northern part of Uganda, and, then later, of the Langi and Acholi who were ethnically closest to him. As already indicated above, this manipulation of the military by Obote led to intra-elite conflicts within both the government and the military and ultimately to Obote's own downfall.

Finally, by building his own personal security force -- the General Service Unit -- in the late 1960s, Obote provoked a measure of apprehension within the regular Uganda Army, whose prestige was threatened. Put together, these subjective methods that Obote utilized to exercise control over the Ugandan military paved the way for the military coup of January 1971 that removed him from power.

Besides his failure to establish effective control over the military, Obote also failed to establish an integrated domestic economy, leading ultimately to further constraints on political order in Uganda, as will be indicated below.

Obote's Policies on the Economy

The economy that Obote's leadership inherited at independence was characterized mainly by two major constraints: structural

111

dependence and domestic inequalities. The concern of this section is to examine the way in which Obote's leadership during the period 1962-1971 responded to these two constraints.

Structural Dependence

Having been developed as a British colony, the Ugandan economy was conditioned, first, to serve British economic interests and, second, to make the colony self-financing. To achieve the former, Uganda was turned into a producer of raw materials, cotton and coffee, for British industry and a market for British industrial products.

Moreover, Uganda's banking system and the bulk of its trade were controlled by foreign interests, including Asian and European firms. And finally, in addition to proceeds from cash-crop exports, poll tax was levied on every adult able-bodied male to raise funds to make the Ugandan economy self-sustaining.

This economic structure hardly changed during Obote's first regime. First, agricultural raw materials continued to constitute more than 85 per cent of Uganda's exports, and still continued to be transformed into finished goods by foreign rather than domestic

112

industry.　Second, foreign firms continued to control most commercial banks, insurance companies, and most of local industry. And finally, Uganda continued to depend mostly on Britain for both export and import trade.　In other words, the post-colonial Ugandan economy continued to be characterized by structural dependence as it had been during the colonial period [41].

Domestic Inequalities

The masses' high expectation of independence turned out to be an illusion.　In order to raise money to pay poll tax, they continued to supply low-paid labor to build the expanding infrastructure of the post-colonial state, and their cash crops continued to sell at low prices.　Meanwhile, their new political masters (the post-colonial African leaders) were busy fashioning networks of patronage and brokerage, as a means to acquire and to sustain themselves in power.　Some of the scarce state resources were utilized by the national leadership to seek political support from local powerful individuals, who themselves used part of the acquired resources to fashion their own patronage.

The majority of the people who were not captured by this extended patron-client relationship remained isolated both politically and economically, with the result that sharp inequalities continued to exist between the leaders and the led. Realizing the mounting popular discontent among the majority of the governed, President Obote made the attempt to reform the system during the late 1960s and the early 1970s. This reform was characterized by two main goals: reducing the level of economic dependence and narrowing the economic gap between leaders and the led.

In the attempt to reduce the level of Uganda's economic dependence, Obote introduced partial nationalization measures on the basis of which the government sought to acquire 60 percent of the shares in major privately-owned firms operating in Uganda, including oil companies, banks, and other credit institutions, insurance companies, bus services, the Kilembe copper mines, manufacturing industries, and major plantations [42].

As it turned out, however, these measures were not implemented consistently. First, some firms were later dropped from the original list of 85, since some of them were either already controlled by the government or were bankrupt by the time these measures were announced by the President. Second, further negotiations between the firms affected and the government led to the revision of the original decision: the formula for oil companies was revised to 50 percent government shares and for some British Banks the formula

was reduced to 40 percent government shares. And finally, negotiations between the government and some of the remaining firms were prolonged up to the time when Obote's
regime was removed from power in a military coup of January 1971.

In his attempt to narrow the economic gap between the governing elites and the governed masses, President Obote sought to reduce the prerogatives and privileges of public servants by (i) abolishing salary increments during the first two years of an employee's probationary period, and introducing bi-annual increments after probation; (ii) abolishing seniority as a basis for promotion; and (iii) abolishing car loans, overtime payments, and all other allowances which were previously enjoyed by Public Servants [43].

However, this policy ignored a number of considerations of which at least three are particularly vital for this discussion. First, neither the army nor the Members of Parliament, including Cabinet Ministers, were affected by this policy. Second, no effort was made by the government either to reduce inequalities between urban centers and rural areas in terms of socio-economic amenities, or to redistribute income between the poor and the rich. And finally, the public servants affected by this new policy, most of whom had

115

previously constituted part of the domestic coalition of the dependent economy in Uganda, regarded the new policy as a major threat to their interests and were, therefore, determined to frustrate its implementation.

Thus, far from promoting bases for political order in Uganda, Obote's abortive economic reforms led to further alienation from his regime of many subgroups in the country.

CONCLUSION

Although the colonial legacy inherited by Obote's leadership at independence was largely responsible for the inter-elite conflict that occurred along the north-south axis during the middle of 1960s, Obote's leadership itself was mainly responsible for most other constraints on political order in Uganda during the period 1962-1971. Obote's failure to acquire legitimacy for his regime led him to depend on coercive military power for his own political survival which, in turn, led to his failure to establish effective control over the military.

Moreover, Obote's abortive economic reforms which failed to establish an integrated domestic economy responsive to the basic human needs of the majority poor, further alienated Obote's leadership from peasants and unskilled workers, at the same time that they provoked resentment from the salariat and foreign commercial strata. A combination of all these constraints ultimately contributed to the downfall of Obote's first regime in a military coup of January 1971.

NOTES

[1] See especially Robert Jackson and Carl Rosberg, "Popular Legitimacy in African Multi-Ethnic States", The Journal of African Studies, 22(June 1984) pp.177-198; and Ruth B. Collier, "Parties, Coups, and Authoritarian Rule: Patterns of Political Change in Tropical Africa", Comparative Political Studies, 11(April 1978) pp.62-93.

[2] For a discussion on personal rule in post-colonial Africa, see especially: Richard Sandbrook and Judith Barker, "Anatomy of Personal Rule", in their The Politics of Africa's Economic Stagnation, London, Cambridge University Press, 1985, pp.89-111; Robert Jackson and Carl Rosberg, Personal Rule in Black Africa, Los Angeles, University of California Press, 1982; and their "Personal Rule: Theory and Practice in Africa", Comparative Politics, 16(July 1984) pp.421-442.

[3] See especially Robert Molteno, "Cleavage and Conflict in Zambia: A Study in Sectionalism," in William Tordoff (ed), Politics in Zambia, London, Manchester University Press, 1974, Chapter 3; Richard Sklar, "Political Science and National Integration -A Radical Approach", Journal of Modern African Studies, 5(1967) pp.1-11.

[4] See especially Claude Welch (ed), Civilian Control of the Military: Theory and Cases from Developing Countries, Albany, State University of New York Press, 1976; and David Goldsworthy, "Civilian Control of the Military in Black Africa", African Affairs, 8(January 1981)pp.49-74.

[5] See especially Joel Samoff, "Class conflict and the State in Africa", Political Science Quarterly, 97(Spring 1982) pp.122-127; and Sandbrook and Barker, The Politics of Africa's Economic Stagnation, pp. 112-144.

[6] See John Cartwright, "Some Constraints Upon African Political Leadership," Canadian Journal of African Studies, 11(1977) pp.435-453, and his Political Leadership in Africa, London and New York, St.Martin's Press, 1983, especially pp.7-18; and Claude Ake, "Explaining Political Instability in New States", Journal of Modern African Studies, 11(1973) pp.347-359.

[7] The alliance was based on the understanding that the UPC would not compete with the KY at least in Buganda. See Hugh Dinwiddy, "The Search for Unity in Uganda: Early Days to 1966," African Affairs, 80 (October 1981) pp.501-518.

[8] 13,602 people voted in favor of a reunion with Bunyoro, and only 3,542 voted in favor of remaining in Buganda. See Ali Mazrui, Violence and Thought: Essays on Social Tensions in Africa, London, Longmans, 1969,p.151.

[9] Ali Mazrui and G.F. Engholm, "Tensions of Crossing the Floor in East Africa", in Ibid, pp.121-146.

[10] This same motion had earlier been rejected by the UPC Parliamentary group for lack of concrete evidence. Obote's opponents, however, changed the Parliamentary programme during the absence of the Prime Minister in order to introduce the motion. See George Kanyeihamba, Constitutional Law and Government in Uganda, Nairobi, East African Literature Bureau, 1975, pp.78-94.

[11] These Cabinet Ministers were: Ibingira, Ngobi, Magezi, Lumu, and Kirya.It was believed that these Ministers together with Edward Mutesa, were involved in a plot to oust Obote from leadership. See especially, Crawford Young, "The Obote Revolution", African Report, 11(June 1966)pp.8-14.

[12] See Edward Mutesa, The Desecration of My Kingdom, London, Constable, 1967, pp.188-189; and Milton Obote, Myths and

Realities: A Letter to a London Friend, Kampala, African Publishers, 1968, p.27.

[13] This commission turned out to be an impartial body of East African Judges: Sir Clement de Lestang of the High Court of Appeal for East Africa; Justice E. Miller, a Judge of the High Court of Kenya; and Justice A. Saidi of the High Court of Tanzania. It found no evidence to implicate Obote and his cabinet colleagues.

[14] The Interim Constitution was adopted by 55 votes in favor and four votes against. See Emory Bundy, "Uganda's New Constitution", East African Journal, 3(June 1966) pp.23-32.

[15] The Kabaka's police and the Baganda ex-service men gave the army some resistance for a complete day, with heavy casualties on both sides, before the palace fell.

[16] See The Republican Constitution of Uganda, Entebbe, Government Printer, 1967, Article 118.

[17] Ibid. Article 80. The four districts into which Buganda was divided included Masaka, Mubende, East Mengo, and West Mengo.

[18] Ibid., Article 24. The President was head of state, head of government, and commander-in-chief of the armed offices. The President also had the power to appoint the Chief Justice of the Uganda High Court, Ibid., Article 84.

[19] G. N. Uzoigwe, "Uganda and Parliamentary Government", Journal of Modern African Studies, 21 (1983) p.265.

[20] These bases of legitimacy are discussed by Max Weber, The Theory of Social Economic Organization, translated by A.M.Henderson and Talcott Parsons, New York, Free Press, 1957, pp.324-363.

[21] According to Deltman, "people of the Third World confer legitimacy upon their political leaders on the basis of their attitudes towards him: that is, upon whether or not he enjoys the support of charismatic norms". Paul Deltman, "Leaders and Structures in Third World Politics: Contrasting Approaches to Legitimacy", Comparative Politics, 6(January 1974) p.268.

[22] Weber, The Theory of Social Economic Organization, pp. 358-359.

[23] Uzoigwe, "Uganda and Parliamentary Government", P.260.

[24] Ali A. Mazuri, "Leadership in Africa: Obote of Uganda", International Journal, 25 (January 1970) p.542.

[25] Sandbrook and Barker, The Politics of Africa's Economic Stagnation, p.84; and Jackson and Rosberg, "Personal Rule: Theory and Practice in Africa", p.421.

[26] See especially Hugh Dinwiddy, "The Uganda Army and Makerere under Obote, 1962-71", African Affairs, 82 (January 1983) pp. 43-59.

[27] For an account on army mutinies in East African states in January 1964, see: "The Brushfire in East Africa", Africa Report, 9 (February 1964) pp.21-24; Special Correspondent, "The Uganda Army: Nexus of Power", Africa Report, 11(December 1966) pp.37-39; and Henry Bienen, "Public Order and the Military in Africa", in Bienen (ed) The Military Intervenes, New York, Russel Sage Foundation, 1968.

[28] Henry Bienen, Armies and Parties in Africa, New York, Africana, 1978, pp.150-160.

[29] The three main demands made by mutineers in the three East African states were (i) wage increases; (ii) rapid Africanization of officer corps; and (iii) promotion of officers from ranks. Uganda met the first demand on a day following the mutiny, by increasing the wages of privates from 105 to 265 Ugandan shillings per month. The other two demands were met within six months following the mutiny.

[30] Special Correspondent, "The Uganda Army: Nexus of Power", P.38.

[31] Ali Mazrui, Soldiers and Kinsmen in Uganda: The Making of A Military Ethnocracy, London, Sage Publications, 1975, P.42; and Uzoigwe, "Uganda and Parliamentary Government", pp.253-271.

[32] As President, Edward Mutesa was the Commander-in-Chief of the Armed Forces of Uganda and, by provisions of the constitution, was supposed to approve any promotions and other changes in the army. See Mutesa, The Desecration of My Kingdom, pp.178-180.

[33] Dinwiddy, "The Search for Unity in Uganda", P.44.

[34] Coming from Teso in eastern Uganda, and having married the daughter of Paulo Kavuma -- ex-Prime Minister of Buganda -- Opolot was believed to have been more sympathetic to Edward Mutesa than he was to Milton Obote during the power struggle between these two personalities. Whether or not this belief was valid, Prime Minister Obote preferred to peg his trust on Idi Amin (a fellow northerner) as the Commander of the Army during the Constitutional Crisis of 1966-67 in Uganda.

[35] See especially David Martin, General Amin, London, Faber and Faber, 1974, pp.67-93; and Bernt Hansen, Ethnicity and Military Rule in Uganda, Uppsala, The Scandinavian Institute of African Studies, 1977, Research Report no.43, pp.89-90.

[36] See especially Mazrui, Soldiers and Kinsmen in Uganda, pp.41-42; and Jan Jorgensen, Uganda: A Modern History, New York, St. Martin's Press, 1981, pp.254-256.

[37] In 1968, Uganda voted in favor of the UN General Assembly Resolution 242, demanding Israel to withdraw from the occupied Arab lands. In the following year, Obote made efforts to improve relations with the Sudan against the wishes of Israel whose policy in the Sudan at the time was to assist the Anya-nya rebels, based

on the Uganda/Sudan border, in order to tie down the Sudanese Army and avoid its involvement in the Israel-Arab conflicts in the Middle East. With the relations between Obote and Israel thus worsening, the latter decided to support Idi Amin in his power struggle with Obote. See especially D.W.Nabudere, Imperialism and Revolution in Uganda, London, Onyx Press, 1980,pp.275-277; and Martin, General Amin, pp.87-89.

[38] According to David Martin, 32 of the 43 officers in the Malire Regiment were either from Amin's home district of West Nile or Nubians, earlier recruited by Amin from the Sudanese refugees in Uganda. Martin, Ibid., pp.154-157.

[39] As indicated in chapter one, Huntington has distinguished two types of leadership control over the military: (i) objective control, which entails the leadership's recognition of an autonomous military professionalism; and (ii) subjective control, which implies the leadership's denial of an independent military sphere. See Samuel Huntington, "Civilian Control of the Military: A Theoretical Statement", in H. Eulau et al., Political Behavior: A Reader in Theory and Research, Glencoe, Free Press, 1956, pp.380-384.

[40] Uzoigwe, "Uganda and Parliamentary Government", p.261. Mazuri seem to agree with Uzoigwe when he argues that "it was

Milton Obote, not Idi Amin, who began the militarization of Uganda's political system". Mazrui, <u>Soldiers and Kinsmen in Uganda</u>, p.139.

[41] See especially: Jorgensen, <u>Uganda: A Modern History</u>, pp.213-266; and Mahmood Mamdani, <u>Class Formation in Uganda</u>, London, Heinemann, 1976, pp.228-301.

[42] These measures were announced by the President in his Labour Day Speech on 1 May 1970, which constitutes Appendix III of Milton Obote, <u>The Common Man's Charter: With Appendices</u>, Entebbe, Government Printer, 1970, pp.41-43.

[43] This policy was contained in the Presidential speech to the Parliament (otherwise known as Communication From the Chair) on 20 April, 1970, which constitutes Appendix II of <u>The Common Man's Charter</u>, pp.23-39.

CHAPTER V

IDI AMIN'S DICTATORIAL RULE (1971-1979)

The study of the role of the military in developing countries has undergone considerable change over the past five decades [1]. The 1950s and early 1960s saw much theorizing about the military as a modernizing agent in developing countries. Not only was the military held to be the most highly organized institution in society, its officer corps were also regarded as being rationally and technologically oriented (variables that measure military professionalism). As well, it gradually became a common belief that the military was insulated from societal tensions, on the ground that it had its distinctive norms that made it identify itself with the nation as whole (variables that measure military corporatism) [2].

Grounded in the orthodox western political tradition, the above theories often distorted more than they explained the evolutionary nature of the military in developing countries. By the late 1960s and early 1970s, when a number of post-colonial states in Africa and Asia were under military rule, scholars began to cast doubts on the actual orientations of militaries in these states toward development.

First, military interventions were explained in terms of internal factionalism existing in their respective societies, from which the military was originally supposed to be insulated. Second, rather than serving as a referee for contending groups within their respective states, empirical evidence indicated that the military had taken power to further the personal welfare of its ranks.

The extension of the military into the economy was seen as having increased the opportunity of its officers to expand their wealth and privilege. And finally, the military, it was noted, required civilian input to serve some functions that the military was either unable or unwilling to perform [3].

By the late 1970s and early 1980s, some scholars seem to have realized the futility of continuing to develop a theory about the development orientation of the military, and turned their attention instead to the study of military regimes in post-colonial states as one of the main sources of dictatorial rule and political disorder [4]. For, during this period, some military regimes that had persisted for about a decade had already brought about a sharp decline of their respective states as reflected, among other things, in: enormous corruption, mal-administration, deterioration of public services, economic decline and the rise of a black market, and arbitrary use of authority by the military to inflict excessive terror on the wider society.

Although these scholars have tended to differ in respect to the conditions under which dictatorial rule emerges and persists in post-colonial states as a whole, they all seem to agree on the basic characteristics of dictatorial rule in the post-colonial states of Africa. The most cited among these basic characteristics included: (i) leaders' severe lack of popular legitimacy, leading them to rely heavily on instruments of coercion (such as the army, secret police, and special forces) as means of enforcing public compliance; (ii) the leaders' tendency to evade constitutional rules, administrative regulations, and other institutional procedures, ultimately leading to political decay; and (iii) the leaders' personalization of state resources, permeated with high levels of patronage linkages and corruption, leading ultimately to the downward spiral of the economy.

The main concern of this chapter is to examine Amin's dictatorial rule in Uganda by focusing, first, on the main conditions under which this type of leadership emerged, second, on the circumstances under which this leadership persisted for nine years despite its colossal brutality against the wider society and, finally, on the extent to which this leadership contributed to the perpetuation and intensification of political disorder in Uganda.

Alternative Sources of Amin's Dictatorial Rule

When Amin and his military supporters came to power after the coup of January 1971, they did not have a ready-made plan to establish highly coercive dictatorial rule in Uganda. But, in their attempt to solve the inherited crises and to establish a political base for their leadership, Amin and his immediate aides ended up by building one of the most highly dictatorial and arbitrary regimes in black Africa to date. In this section, I will first discuss the main elements of the legacy inherited by Amin's leadership and then examine the main methods utilized by this leadership to perpetuate its own political base.

(i) **Inherited Legacy**: As Claude Welch has correctly argued, "members of the armed forces cannot successfully usurp control, over an extended period, from a government considered legitimate by the populace" [5]. Hence, one of the legacies inherited by Amin's leadership was a crisis of legitimacy, which had persisted under the previous Obote leadership. In particular, since the crisis of legitimacy of the previous regime arose partly from the excesses committed by the army that Amin commanded, the challenge that Amin faced as a new leader was how he could acquire popular legitimacy for his regime in the light of his past record.

Secondly, at the time Amin took over power, not only was the Uganda Army still unbalanced in favor of the northern region, but it was also still divided along sectional lines: the Langi and Acholi soldiers who had been favored by Obote on the one hand and soldiers from West Nile, who had felt deprived during the previous regime, on the other. Amin's challenge was the extent to which he could unite these factions within the army behind his leadership.

Finally, Amin, like Obote before him, inherited a dependent economy that was characterized by domestic inequalities and external control. Amin's challenge was how he could establish an integrated domestic economy that was responsive to local needs.

In response to these three main challenges inherited from the previous regime, Amin acted swiftly. In the attempt to regain the confidence and support of the Baganda, who had suffered most from excesses committed by the Uganda Army during the previous Obote regime, Amin not only lifted the state of emergency that had been declared over Buganda since the 1966 constitutional crisis, but he also brought back the body of the Kabaka from Britain (where the latter had died in exile in 1969) for a state funeral. Amin also released political detainees most of whom were prominent Baganda. In the rest of Uganda, Amin granted separate districts to those ethnic groups which had demanded them in vain during the previous regime, and established councils of elders in each district throughout Uganda, consisting of local notables whom he instructed to channel grievances arising from their respective districts directly to him [6].

However, the manner in which Amin decided to resolve the other two challenges clearly marked the beginning of his dictatorial rule. First, instead of reconciling differences between the two major factions within the army, Amin decided to eliminate the Langi and Acholi soldiers altogether through a systematic purge [7]. Second, Amin expelled all Asian commercial strata from the country and then later nationalized most of the foreign firms operating in Uganda, without providing them with compensation [8].

(ii) The Search for Loyalty: Given the fact that hardly any regime can survive for long unless it acquires some support from society, Amin sought to establish a social base for his regime at the same time that he searched for personal loyalty within sectors of government.

Following the expulsion of Asians from Uganda, Amin utilized the businesses and properties they left behind to seek support for his leadership. Initially the Asian property was distributed to Ugandan businessmen and women who were thought to be capable of running the economy efficiently.

This assumption was ill conceived on at least two accounts. First, foreign companies from which most imports could be purchased did not trust their new agents in Uganda and as such most international transactions had to be in cash rather than on letters of credit. And second, most of the Ugandans who inherited Asian businesses sought to earn handsome profits in the shortest time possible and, lacking foreign currency with which they could buy new stock of goods, they began to hoard essential commodities which they later sold at uncontrolled prices in the black market (commonly known as "magendo" trade in Uganda). In most shops, the stock was run down to zero and then abandoned.

By the middle of the 1970s, the scarcity of commodities had already led to very high prices that, in turn, led Amin to declare that overcharging and hoarding were to be treated as acts of treason, and that anybody found guilty of either of these acts was to face a firing squad [9]. Thus what had started as a search for leadership's support was now turning into a new source of conflict between the leadership and the business community.

A second method utilized by Amin to establish a social base for his regime was the manipulation of religious differences in Uganda. Islam, Amin's religion that nevertheless had a membership of less than 10 percent of Uganda's population, was turned into a semi-official religion, at the same time that other religions in Uganda were alienated by Amin's leadership. Amin allocated land and part of the abandoned Asian businesses and properties to the Uganda Muslim Supreme Council. By the middle of 1970s, this Council controlled all mosques in the country, many housing estates, schools, and a number of factories. The proceeds from some of these assets, in addition to some funds donated by Islamic countries (notably Libya) were to be used for purposes of conversions to Islam, building more mosques and schools and, in the long run, establishing an Islamic University in Uganda. To further these goals, Arabic broadcasts were introduced on both radio and television, and Arabic was made one of the languages on Ugandan passports.

However, this method of seeking a social base for Amin's leadership was also ill conceived. First, most of tangible resources provided to the Muslim community ended up in the hands of the upper echelons of the Muslim Supreme Council, leaving hardly anything for the rank and file of the larger Muslim community. And second, even if all Muslims supported Amin's leadership on the basis of religious affiliation, such support would not have outweighed the frustration and resentment among Christians whose membership was well over 70 percent of the Ugandan population [10]. Faced with these and other related constraints, Idi Amin decided to militarize the Ugandan system as an alternative means to sustain his leadership.

The Militarization of the Ugandan System

Having come to power without a popular mandate from the governed and having tried in vain to win popular legitimacy through the methods mentioned above, Amin and his immediate aides decided to militarize the Ugandan system by seeking to establish direct military control over the main socio-economic and political sectors in the country. This process began within government sectors and then later spread to the wider society.

(i) **The Militarization of the State**: Following brutal purges of the Langi and Acholi soldiers as well as other security personnel within the police, who were considered to be dissidents by the leadership, Amin's regime recruited mercenaries from southern Sudan, eastern Zaire, and from the urban unemployed into the Ugandan security forces. In addition to swelling the ranks of the Uganda Army, a significant number of these new recruits were placed in two "intelligence-gathering" units of Amin's regime: the State Research Bureau and the Public Safety Unit, both of which were endowed with state power to penetrate Ugandan society, including the army, the police, the civil service, and the wider public.

In addition, Amin's cabinet which initially was predominantly civilian in membership was later recomposed to consist mainly of military officers and subordinated to the Defense Council which itself was dominated by Amin [11].

Moreover, in further attempts to militarize the government sector, Amin sought to reduce the powers of the judiciary. The conflict between Amin and the judiciary came to a head in September 1972, when the then Chief Justice of Uganda, Benedicto Kiwanuka, who had also been the Chief Minister of Uganda prior to independence was dragged from his chambers by military men and

138

later killed. Early the following year, Decree 3 of 1973 was proclaimed by Amin. It provided military tribunals with formal powers to try civilian offenders, including among others: political prisoners, those accused of hoarding and selling commodities at uncontrolled prices, and any woman accused of having an abortion. In all essentials, therefore, military tribunals took over from civilian courts those cases that were considered by the government as involving "crimes against the state" [12].

The local government system in the country was also militarized. The regime created 10 provinces out of the pre-existing four, each of which was headed by a military Provincial Governor. Within each Province there were a number of districts, which were headed mostly by military District Commissioners. County and Sub-county Chiefs were also appointed by the military government and most of them were military officers. Only parish chiefs were "elected" by the governed, but these elections were supervised by military personnel who, however, had a final say in deciding who was to be the chief, the results of the election notwithstanding [13].

Finally, most state corporations were put under the directorship of military officers, most of who were not competent enough to direct them efficiently [14]. The only sector of the state that generally remained unmilitarized was the top echelon of the civil service, comprising Permanent Secretaries and their immediate subordinates. But even here, those who served in Ministries headed by ill-educated Military officers were quite often accused of misleading their Ministers with the supposed intention of making them look stupid in public. This negative attitude towards these high level civil servants resulted in an unusually high rate of dismissal within their ranks.

(ii) The Militarization of the Economy: Amin's militarization of the Ugandan economy was carried out simultaneously with his militarization of the state. In order to analyze the extent to which the Ugandan economy was militarized during Amin's leadership, at least three factors are particularly vital: (a) the vast expenditure on the military; (b) the manner in which businesses and properties left behind by expelled Asians were ultimately redistributed; and (c) the extent to which economic planning was de-emphasized during Amin's leadership. I will discuss these factors in turn.

Within his first year in office, Amin increased military expenditure by well over 50 percent of the pre-coup government estimates for the Ministry of Defense [15]. In subsequent years, Uganda's military expenditure continued to rise at a very high rate. This ever-increasing military expenditure was not only spent on military hardware, but also on the importation of goods for the expanding armed forces. For the year 1971, Uganda's imports increased by 20 percent at the same time that exports declined by 9 percent, leading to a trade deficit of 43 million Ugandan shillings, the highest deficit since Uganda's independence [16].

Meanwhile, government's borrowing from the Bank of Uganda also increased from 103 million Ugandan shillings at the time of the coup (in January 1971) to about 1000 million Ugandan shillings at the end of that year [17].

Amin's vast expenditure on the military exhausted the foreign exchange earned from exports, leaving hardly any resources for manufacturing industries, which depended on imports for spare parts and raw materials. With manufacturing production thus declining Amin ordered more money to be printed, reducing thereby the purchasing power of the shilling. As a result of this extravagant policy, there developed an inflationary spiral in Uganda.

The lower-income groups, who were hit hardest by this astronomical inflation, reacted by organizing strikes and even sabotage in industries where they worked. Amin reacted by sending armed forces to "discipline" workers whenever there was a strike in any big industry, leading to a migration of workers from towns to the countryside.

The countryside itself also suffered from the impact of this inflation. Peasants paid much more for the few commodities they purchased and were paid less for the cash crops they produced. The peasants' response was to abandon cash-crop production in favour of producing food crops, whose prices they could themselves determine [18].

With the subsequent sharp decline in export crop production, Amin's government reacted by: (a) calling upon Provincial Governors to enforce sustained production of cash crops using any means, military or otherwise; and (b) introducing a Land Reform Decree of June 1975, on the basis of which all land in Uganda became state property. The Land Commission that was appointed to implement this decree, was given power to terminate any lease on "undeveloped" land and to grant it to a potential developer [19].

Following this decree, high level government officials together with rich business personnel, especially those with military connections, grabbed land from peasants some of whom were subsequently made homeless.

In his further attempts to militarize the Ugandan economy, Amin expelled the Asian commercial strata in Uganda and gave their businesses and properties, first, to the general business community in Uganda and then, later, to his military officers. The former were accused of hoarding and overcharging, and the military was set in motion to clamp down on traders who hoarded and/or overcharged. In 1975, the Economic Crimes Tribunal Decree set up military tribunals in each province with exclusive powers to try those involved in hoarding and overcharging, and to reallocate the businesses of those found guilty of such crimes. By 1977 most businesses in Uganda had been reallocated to soldiers, and in June of that year Amin declared that businessmen were free to buy and fix prices for their commodities, arguing that prices would automatically drop when the market was flooded with commodities [20].

However, with a sharp decline in industrial production due to poor management and a general lack of spare parts for the machinery, the few commodities produced were distributed among military businessmen who subsequently fixed their prices at will in the black market trade.

The expulsion of Asians from Uganda and the subsequent mismanagement of the businesses they left behind led to far-reaching repercussions for the country as a whole. Three of these repercussions are particularly vital for this discussion. First, most industries run by Asians had been particularly efficient and productive since Asian business agents had already established connections within the international economy. It would have required a gradual and/or piecemeal process to train Ugandans and to allow them to acquire the expertise necessary to run the economy smoothly before Asian agents were expelled.

Second, not all Asians in Uganda were involved in business. Some of them were teachers, doctors, civil servants and the like. The abrupt expulsion of such professionals robbed the country of vital talent necessary for development, especially since some of these Asians were Ugandan citizens and committed to the development of the country.

Finally, although the Africanization of the Ugandan economy could have been beneficial to Ugandans in the long run, the manner in which it was carried out by Amin turned out to be dysfunctional. Soldiers who ultimately became the main beneficiaries of the Asian businesses lacked any skills in running them. In particular, since these soldiers were running the affairs of the state on a full-time basis, their commercial businesses were run by family members (wives, mothers, sisters, brothers and the like) most of whom could only speak their local languages, thereby narrowing the level of communication between customers and business attendants.

On the basis of the foregoing, it is clear that Amin ran the Ugandan economy, and indeed the country as a whole, as if it was a family affair. Not only was Amin's administration highly personal in a sense that he made most government decisions without consulting anybody, including both the cabinet and the defense council, but it was also permeated with patronage and corruption. Given the radical economic reforms attempted by Amin's military regime, the input of educated elites in planning the future trend of the economy would have been particularly necessary. However, Amin's twin policies of alienating the educated wherever possible and of promoting his unlettered social peers from the military to positions of power and authority, ultimately led to the downward spiral of the Ugandan economy.

Anatomy of Political Decay

Reduced to its basic essentials, Amin's leadership in Uganda promoted nothing more than national political and economic decay. In this section an attempt will be made to elaborate on this evaluation of Amin's Leadership. Operationally defined in terms of such indicators as erosion of representative political institutions, political instability, deterioration of administrative capacity, deterioration of public services, corruption within the ranks of government, random violence, and a high level of indiscipline within the armed forces [21], political decay was a characteristic feature of Amin regime. I will discuss some of these indicators in relation to Amin's leadership.

(i) **Erosion of Representative Institutions**: Within a week after he had taken power in a coup, Amin dissolved the national Parliament and assumed both legislative and executive powers, declaring that he would henceforth rule by decree. His first two decrees, both announced on 2 February 1971, were, first, the Armed Forces Decree providing for the establishment of a Defense Council, chaired by Amin himself and composed of an unspecified number of soldiers and, second, the Local Administrations and Urban Authorities Decree, dissolving representative councils in all districts,

146

municipalities and towns [22]. Thus within less than two weeks of his leadership, Amin had already terminated all major representative political institutions in Uganda.

(ii) Political Instability: The most cited composite indicators of political instability include: (a) turmoil, which involves such incidents as riots, demonstrations, and strikes; (b) communal violence, involving civil wars, rebellions, and inter-ethnic conflicts; and (c) elite instability, which involves coups, attempted coups, and other forms of inter- and intra-elite conflicts [23].

In less than a year following Amin's coup, workers in major industries and firms throughout Uganda had already staged strikes, demanding better pay to match the inflationary spiral already in motion. A string of these strikes was started by workers at Kampala City Counci, in September 1971 [24]. By the end of that year there were strikes in several of the major industries in the country, including: Lugazi sugar cane plantation, Jinja Garments Industry, and Kilembe Copper Mines. After Amin had sent the military to restore order at the above sites, albeit through brutality, he declared that his government would no longer tolerate any more "illegal" strikes [25], and from then onwards strikes were banned in Uganda.

The only group that ventured to demonstrate against Amin's increasingly repressive regime was Makerere University students [26]. On 6 March 1976, Paul Serwanga who was a law student from Makerere University was shot and killed by Amin's soldiers just outside the gates of the university. Following this incident, students took to the streets to demonstrate against such brutality. In early August, in the same year, university students boycotted lectures and demanded that Amin's son should be removed from the campus immediately.

Although Amin's son was not a regular university student as such, having been brought to university to take some lessons in languages, he was allocated a personal flat in one hall of residence while other undergraduate students were sharing rooms. As well, he carried a gun with him all the time and had already threatened to shoot a member of faculty for having refused him entry into the university faculty club. Amin's reaction towards the demonstration against his son was to send armed soldiers to the campus, who subsequently rounded up students and took them to army barracks for torture, rape, and other forms of brutality.

Throughout Amin's leadership there were many attempted palace coups most of which went unpublished. Among those which were noticed included the one spearheaded by Ondoga (then Minister of Foreign Affairs) in early1974, who subsequently was murdered together with a number of soldiers from his Lugbara ethnic group; and another spearheaded by Charles Arube, then Chief of Staff of the Armed Forces, who was also subsequently murdered by Amin [27].

Having terrorized all strata of Ugandan society, the only challenge to Amin's leadership could be organized outside Uganda. The Langi and Acholi soldiers who managed to escape Amin's purges of the early 1970s fled to Tanzania where, together with some other Ugandan exiles, began to organize a guerrilla force to invade Amin's Uganda. The first invasion by this group in September 1972 was easily repulsed by Amin's troops. However, Amin used this invasion as an excuse, first, for bombing Tanzanian villages at the border between Tanzania and Uganda and, second, for purging most prominent politicians in Uganda. Early in 1973, Amin paraded prominent former supporters of Obote at their respective district headquarters throughout Uganda and executed them publicly. The pretext for this massacre was that the victims had conspired with pro-Obote supporters who had invaded Uganda in September 1972 [28].

149

The second major invasion on Amin's Uganda was also organized in Tanzania and was heavily supported by the latter's troops. To distract his army from its internal divisions (there was a growing division between soldiers loyal to Amin and those loyal to vice President Adrisi Mustafa), Amin sent troops to attack Tanzania in October 1978, under the pretext that Tanzania was training guerrillas to attack Uganda. In retaliation against Amin's aggression, President Nyerere of Tanzania sent his own troops to back up decisively a guerrilla force composed of Ugandan exiles to invade Uganda, and by April 1979, a combination of these forces had succeeded in removing Amin from power.

(iii) Deterioration of Administrative Capacity: Bureaucratic institutions in Uganda began to deteriorate during the early years of Amin's leadership. Among the many factors that may have been responsible, at least four of them seem to have been particularly prominent. First, Amin's policies of recruitment and promotion within these institutions were primarily based on two criteria: nepotism and patronage, with a result that bureaucratic ranks were gradually filled with incompetents. Second, most of Amin's civilian cabinet ministers were drawn from the top echelons of the Public Service, leaving their respective institutions without adequate leadership. In addition, Amin dismissed 22 Senior Civil Servants in

April 1972 of whom 10 were Permanent Secretaries [29]. Third, as the spiral of inflation deepened, most of the well-qualified public servants fled the country in search of alternative employment abroad. Finally, systematic corruption which was initially introduced by Amin's new appointees, spread throughout the bureaucratic ranks with the result that the few remaining competent and honest public servants became demoralized.

The deterioration of administrative capacity coupled with shortage of imports and very low productive capacity of local industries led to deterioration of public services. Hospitals and other health centres suffered from a severe shortage of drugs. University and schools lacked both textbooks and stationery. Roads were everywhere full of pot holes. Public transport was reduced to a bare minimum because of a shortage of spare parts. Food in cities and town became expensive due to high transportation costs. And due to the shortage of vehicles and manpower, on the part of Kampala City Council, the smell from uncollected sewage polluted the air in the capital city.

(iv) Indiscipline Within the Armed Forces: Having purged the Langi and Acholi soldiers, who had previously constituted the core of the Uganda Army, Amin hurriedly recruited new soldiers from

Anyanya rebels of southern Sudan and others from eastern Zaire. These mercenary troops together with a group of soldiers who were recruited from among the unemployed, were given state powers to permeate the entire Ugandan society. As early as March 1971, two months after Amin had taken over power, an Armed Forces (Powers of Arrest) Decree was promulgated by Amin, granting soldiers the power to search and arrest any suspected dissident. With this decree in place, new recruits into the army prospered from thefts and extortions under the guise of searching for dissidents. Any rich person that did not have military connections was labeled a dissident and searched until his entire property, and in most cases his own life, was taken away. As well, new recruits into the regular army were commonly hired by individuals to help them settle scores with their enemies. The officers on the other hand grew rich by "controlling" the smuggling of coffee to neighbouring countries and by inheriting most of the assets left behind by expelled Asians.

CONCLUSION

On the basis of the preceding discussion, it is clear that Amin's dictatorial rule in Uganda affected almost every aspect of society. It uprooted a large segment of the population into exile, exacerbated both economic inequalities and social conflict, and left the country with a legacy of economic collapse, bankruptcy, social strife and political decay. The optimism that surrounded much of the earlier theory on the positive role of the military in developing countries was based primarily on the assumption that militaries in these countries were characterized by both professionalism and corporatism -- the two main criteria on the basis of which military efficiency in the industrialized world is measured. This assumption, however, ignored two crucial factors. First, not all militaries have the same internal characteristics in relation to education and training to enable them to have the ability to limit their political role to expert advice on strictly military issues. And second, different militaries interact with their societies in different ways depending, among other things, on the criteria on the basis of which they are recruited and promoted, and the method utilized by their respective governments to establish control over them.

While the colonial power attempted to establish objective control over its militaries, along similar lines as those which existed in the metropole, post-colonial leadership particularly in Africa sought to reverse the system by biasing both recruitment and promotion policies in favor of those who were ethnically kin to politically dominant groups, thereby limiting chances for the development of military corporatism. Having inherited Obote's legacy of maintaining ethnic imbalances within the Ugandan armed forces in favor of northern Uganda, Amin took a step further by recruiting and promoting mercenary soldiers from southern Sudan and north-eastern Zaire, who nonetheless were ethnically close to Amin since his home borders these two areas.

Moreover, Amin's lack of respect for military professionalism was reflected, among other things, in his utilization of the armed forces to carry out wide-scale violence and routine massacres as an alternative means of social control.

NOTES

[1] For a concise account about this change see especially Henry Bienen, "Armed Forces and Modernization: Continuing the Debate", Comparative Politics, 16(October 1983) pp.1-16.

[2] See especially: contributions to the volume edited by J. Johnson, The Role of the Military in Underdeveloped Countries, Princeton, Princeton University Press, 1962; Hans Daalder, The Role of the Military in the Emerging Countries, The Hague, Mouton, 1962; and Morris Janowitz, The Military in the Political Development of New Nations, Chicago, University of Chicago Press, 1964.

[3] For these and other related doubts about the military in post-colonial states, see especially: Kenneth Grundy, Conflicting Images of the Military in Africa, Nairobi, East African Publishing House, 1968; Claude Welch (ed), Soldiers and State in Africa: A Comparative Analysis of Military Intervention and Change, Evanston, Northwestern University Press, 1970; William Gutteridge, "Opportunism and Military interventions in Black Africa, East African Journal, 9 (September 1972) pp.8-18; and Robert Pinkney, "The

Theory and Practice of Military Government", Political Studies, 21(June 1973) pp.152-166.

[4] See especially: Samuel Decalo, "African Personal Dictatorships", Journal of Modern African Studies, 23(1985) pp.209-237; Cynthia Enloe, Police, Military and Ethnicity: The Foundation of State Power, New Brunswick, Transaction Books, 1980; Thomas Callaghy, The State-Society Struggle: Zaire in Comparative Perspective, New York, Columbia University Press, 1984, especially pp.3-79; Richard Sandbrook and Judith Barker, The Politics of Africa's Economic Stagnation, London, Cambridge University Press, 1985, especially pp.83-111; Robert Jackson and Carl Rosberg, Personal Rule in Black Africa: Prince, Autocrat, Prophet, Tyrant , Los Angeles, University of California Press, 1982; and Ruth Collier, "Parties, Coups, and Authoritarian Rule: Patterns of Political Change in Tropical Africa", Comparative Political Studies, 11(April 1978) pp.62-93.

[5] Claude Welch (ed), Civilian Control of the Military: Theory and Cases from Developing Countries, Albany, State University of New York Press, 1976, P.323.

[6] It should be noted that Amin established these councils of elders to replace the existing elected District Councils that he abolished on 2 February, 1971, through the Local Administration and Urban Authorities Decree. This decree dissolved District, Municipal and Town Councils. The composition of Councils of Elders were not elected but hand-picked by Amin, who used them to justify some of the policies he adopted, claiming that he had been advised by these councils to do so.

[7] See especially "Inside Amin's Uganda: More Africans Murdered", Munger Africana Library Notes, 18(March 1973) pp.1-22; and David Martin, General Amin, London, Faber and Faber, 1974, pp.130-157.

[8] About the expulsion of Asians from Uganda, see especially Yash Tandon, "The Asians in East Africa in 1972", in C. Legum (ed), Africa Contemporary Record Volume 5 1972-1973, London, pp.A3-19; and Ali Mazrui, "The De-Indianization of Uganda: Who is a Citizen?", in David Smock and K.Bentsi-Enchill (eds), The Search for National Integration in Africa, London, The Free Press, 1975, pp.68-76. In addition to expelling Asians, Amin nationalized some British companies without compensation through the Properties and Business (Acquisition) Decree of December 18, 1972.

[9] The Voice of Uganda, January 9, 1975. The Voice of Uganda was a government newspaper that replaced the old Uganda Argus in 1973.

[10] Uganda is composed of over 70 percent Christians, less than 10 percent Muslims. The rest do not have any modern religious affiliations and, in the view of most Christians and Muslims, are regarded as "pagans".

[11] Although the Defense Council was established by Amin's first decree (Armed Forces Decree) on 2 February, 1971, its membership was never made public. It was chaired by Amin himself but whoever composed it was kept a secret for unknown reasons.

[12] During Amin's regime, top positions in the judiciary were filled with foreigners mainly Muslims from Pakistan. After killing Kiwanuka, Mohamed Saied from Pakistan was made the Chief Justice. A number of Judges both in the High Court and within districts were recruited from Pakistan. These Judges, however, handled petty cases leaving the important ones to be handled by Military Tribunals.

[13] I personally witnessed a case where people voted for a Parish Chief and his assistant. Among the contenders for these two positions were a son and his father both of whom lost the election. However, the soldier who supervised this election was ethnically related to this family. He ended up giving these positions to the family members. The son was made the Parish Chief and his father the assistant.

[14] The largest industrial enterprises in Uganda, including the Coffee Marketing Board, Uganda Transport Company, Lugazi Sugar Factory and many others were directed by military officers. Amin himself became chairman of Kilembe Copper Mines and appointed Major Galla as his managing director.

[15] See The Appropriation Decree Nos.23 and 35 (1971), 15 and 16(1972), Entebbe, Government Printer, 1971 and 1972.

[16] See Mahmood Mamdani, Imperialism and Fascism in Uganda, Nairobi, Heinemann Educational Books, 1983, pp.47-48.

[17] "Inside Amin's Uganda", pp.12-13.

[18] This type of peasant behavior is typical in African economies. Goran Hyden's thesis of "uncaptured peasantry" focuses on the ability of Tanzanian peasantry to veto unpopular state policies by withdrawing into subsistence agriculture. Building on Hyden's thesis, Stephen Bunker's study of Bugisu District in eastern Uganda examines responses of coffee growers in that district towards state policies during Obote's second term of office (1980-1985). See Goran Hyden, Beyond Ujamaa in Tanzania: Underdevelopment and Uncaptured Peasantry, Berkeley, University of California Press, 1980; and Stephen G.Bunker, "Peasant Responses to a Dependent State: Uganda, 1983" Canadian Journal of African Studies, 19(1985) pp.371-386.

[19] See The Voice of Uganda, June 2, 1975.

[20] The Voice of Uganda, June 17, 1977.

[21] The concept of political decay derives from Huntington who discusses most of these indicators. See Samuel Huntington, "Political Development and Political Decay", World Politics, 17(April 1965) pp.386-430.

[22] Uganda Argus, February 3, 1971.

[23] See especially Donald Morrison, et al, Black Africa: A Comparative Handbook, New York, The Free Press, 1972, pp.128-130.

[24] Uganda Argus, September 18, 1971.

[25] Uganda Argus, December 23, 1971.

[26] For a detailed account on demonstrations by Makerere University Students against Amin's regime, see Bryan Langlands, "Students and Politics in Uganda", African Affairs, 76 (January 1977) pp.3-20.

[27] See "General Amin's Uganda", Africa Contemporary Record Current Affairs Series, London, Rex Collings, 1974, pp.7-16.

[28] See David Martin, General Amin, pp.211-230.

[29] Uganda Argus, April 21, 1972. The remaining part of this section is based mainly on keen observation of Amin's leadership by the author, first, as a student of political science at Makerere University and, later, as an instructor at the same university.

CHAPTER VI

POST-AMIN LEADERSHIP

In this chapter, which draws on Uganda's experience in reconstituting civilian leadership following an abrupt forceful removal of Amin's military rule in April 1979, I will examine post-Amin regimes with a view to identifying the main constraints on political order and re-integration in Uganda during this period.

In particular, leadership performance of each of these regimes will be assessed on the basis of at least three types of government policies: (i) economic policies, evaluating the extent to which these leaders attempted to rehabilitate the country's economy; (ii) security policies, examining the attempt made by these leaders to re-establish political order and internal security; and (iii) administrative policies, analyzing the extent to which these leaders were successful in acquiring popular legitimacy and in overcoming problems arising from sectionalism. First, however, it appears appropriate to provide an overview of the background to these regimes.

The 28 Ugandan exile groups who were represented at the meeting held in the northern Tanzania town of Moshi from 24 to 26 March

1979 [1], made at least four major decisions. First, they constituted themselves into the Uganda National Liberation Front (UNLF), responsible for the overthrow of Idi Amin's regime. Second, they elected an Executive Council to lead the Front, composed of 11 people under the chairmanship of Yusuf Lule -- former Vice-Chancellor of Makerere University. Third, they elected members of the National Consultative Council (NCC), composed of one member from each of the 28 groups represented at the meeting, as well as the Chairman and Secretary for this Council [2]. And finally, they appointed members of three commissions: (i) the Political and Diplomatic Commission; (ii) the Finance and Administration Commission; and (iii) the Military Commission.

However, less attention was paid to a clear-cut division of power between the Chairman of the Executive Council who was later to occupy the institution of the Presidency and the NCC that was later to assume legislative powers. The ambiguity that surrounded power sharing between these institutions together with Amin's legacy, ultimately led to a number of constraints as will be indicated below.

Amin's Legacy

There were at least three types of problems inherited from Amin's regime. First, the regime had brought the country's economy to a virtual standstill. In particular, there was a severe shortage of all essential commodities, equipment, spare parts and most consumer goods, with the result that the black market and smuggling were institutionalized.

Second, the new civilian government inherited serious security problems partly from Amin's violent military rule and partly from the war of liberation. The liberating forces had emptied prisons in Uganda, thereby releasing not only political victims but also hardened criminals. As well, there were many weapons unaccounted for in the country, mostly thrown away by Amin's fleeing soldiers, many of whom were themselves still at large.

And finally, administrative structures were also in ruins. Amin's arbitrary rule had demoralized civil servants, and links between the centre and localities had also broken down. Since the 10 provinces and 38 districts created by Idi Amin had been headed by military Governors and District Commissioners, respectively, Amin's overthrow left the new civil administration with no communication channels between the centre in Kampala and the rural localities [3].
165

Thus, immediately after the overthrow of Amin, the Ugandan system was more disintegrated than ever before. There was both an institutional and a political vacuum, coupled with a state of anarchy as reflected in widespread looting, rape, and armed robberies.

It is against this background that the first post-Amin regime, under the leadership of Yusuf Lule, should be examined.

Yusuf Lule's Leadership (April- June 1979)

Immediately following the liberation of Kampala, civilian rule was restored when Lule and his Cabinet were sworn into office on 13 April 1979 [4]. In this section I will discuss the extent to which Lule's short-lived administration attempted to respond to the problems that it inherited.

(i) Lule's Economic Policies: Lule's leadership was generally regarded as pro-Western in its economic orientation, and hence provoked criticisms for its failure to establish a mixed economic policy which had earlier been recommended by the Commonwealth team of experts [5].

Even more crucial was the manner in which Lule's regime distributed businesses and properties abandoned by Amin's soldiers and supporters who had fled the country for fear of reprisal. Some members of the UNLF made public charges against Lule personally that the manner in which he distributed these businesses and properties reflected elements of corruption since his close associates, especially from among his fellow Baganda, were taking a lion's share in this distribution [6]. In that respect, Lule's redistribution of abandoned businesses and properties was not much different from that of Amin, who previously had re-allocated businesses and properties abandoned by expelled Asians to his closest ethnic associates, mostly from the army, as indicated in chapter six.

Hence, during Lule's short-lived regime, Uganda's economy continued to decline since hardly any effort was made either to curb the existing inflation or to eliminate the black market.

(ii) Lule's Security Policies: Lule's security policies, with their emphasis on the establishment of a literate army which was also representative of the country as a whole, differed significantly from those of his predecessors. Both the colonial administration and Obote's first regime had each recruited a northern-dominated army, which was also largely illiterate. While maintaining similar policies, Amin took a step even further by recruiting mercenaries from southern Sudan and north-eastern Zaire, who were largely illiterate and ethnically close to him.

However, Lule's policy of reconstituting security forces on the basis of proportional regional representation aroused fears among some Ugandans. These fears were mainly based on the view that proportional regional recruitment into the army would ultimately favor Buganda whose population, as a single regional entity, was bigger than any other region in the country [7].

In any event, Lule lost political power before his security policies were implemented, and during his leadership neither political order nor internal security was restored.

(iii) Lule's Administrative Policies: Lule's cabinet was internally divided right from the start. At least three divisions within it were apparent. First, Lule's inner circle of advisers, who included Sam Sebagereka, Martin Aliker, Semei Nyanzi, and Robert Serumaga, were all regarded as supporters of Western style economic development. Second, there was a radical group in the cabinet which included the Minister of Defense, Yoweri Museveni, the

Minister of Justice, Dan Nabudere, and Ateke Ejalu who was the Minister of Information. And finally, there was a group who were regarded as Obote supporters. This group included the Minister of Foreign Affairs, Otema Alimadi, the Minister of Energy and Communication, Aken P'Jock, and Paulo Muwanga who was Minister of Internal Affairs [8].

However, what ultimately became a source of serious conflicts between Lule and the National Consultative Council (NCC) was Lule's assumption of executive powers based on the 1967 Republic Constitution of Uganda which, as indicated in chapter five, endowed the Presidency with excessive powers. This conflict came to a head in June 1979, when Lule reshuffled his cabinet without consulting the NCC. The ministers affected accused Lule of using dictatorial methods in carrying out cabinet reshuffles with the intention of putting his supporters in key positions [9]. And on 20 June 1979, the Chairman of the NCC, Edward Rugumayo, announced that Yusuf Lule had been dismissed as the President of Uganda for ignoring democratic methods in making decisions of vital significance to the nation, including the appointment and reshuffling of cabinet ministers without consulting the NCC or any other organs of the UNLF, the arbitrary reorganization of local administrative structures, and undemocratic procedures in the allocation and reallocation of businesses [10]. There was also a latent fear that Lule intended ultimately to restore monarchism in Uganda [11].

Amin's legacy, critical though it was, seems not to have been solely responsible for the fall of Lule's regime. In theory, a successful return to civilian leadership after a period of military rule requires, among other things, the ability of civilian leaders to govern and to re-establish their legitimacy [12].

Lule's regime fell short of these expectations mainly in three ways. First, Lule's distribution of abandoned businesses and properties to his closest friends eroded the credibility of his leadership. Second, Lule's failure to establish civil order in the country, coupled with his revival of the unpopular Republican Constitution of 1967 as a basis of his leadership, seriously undermined legitimacy for his regime. And finally, the struggle for power within the ranks of the UNLF constrained decision-making at the centre, thereby making the regime as a whole less effective in tackling the country's numerous problems.

Unfortunately, similar constraints that led to Lule's downfall in the middle of 1979 were also largely responsible for the fall of his successor hardly a year later, as will be indicated below.

Binaisa's Leadership (June 1979- May 1980)

Following Lule's dismissal, the NCC held a meeting and appointed Godfrey Binaisa as the next President. While Binaisa retained some of the Cabinet Ministers that had served under Yusuf Lule, he replaced the latter's strong supporters with his own supporters [13].

(i) Binaisa's economic policies: Binaisa's stated economic policy was based primarily on a mixed economy where both foreign and domestic interests were free to establish private enterprises. At the same time the government, with the help of the international community, would make every attempt to assist local farmers and peasants to develop the agricultural economy. However, the problem of distributing abandoned businesses and properties took a new turn during Binaisa's leadership. Ugandans who had stayed and suffered under Amin's rule increasingly resented the redistribution procedure, arguing that returning exiles were taking the lion's share. Binaisa's regime responded by establishing the National Renting and Allocation Board in the middle of October 1979, which subsequently became responsible for redistribution [14].

However, Uganda's economy during Binaisa's leadership was no better than it had been during Lule's regime. Shortages of essential commodities, inflation, and the black market trade continued to rise.

(ii) Binaisa's Administrative Policies: Skillfully seeking to neutralize the powerful NCC, Binaisa's regime increased NCC's membership from thirty to 127 in October 1979. Sixty- one of the new members were elected by District Electoral Colleges which were nominated by Binaisa's Minister of Local Government, and then approved by the existing NCC. As well, ten of the new members were selected from the UNLF Army by the Defense Minister, Yoweri Museveni, while the remaining twenty six were chosen from among other UNLF members [15].

However, elections for the sixty-one members of the NCC revived cleavages and rivalries at the district level, which were reminiscent of factional politics in Uganda during the 1950s and 1960s, as indicated in chapters four and five. Accusations were made that the results of district elections were biased against Catholics and non-members of the UPC [16].

The irony of this accusation, however, was that Binaisa's regime had reorganized the country into thirty- two new districts before these elections were held, arguing that old district units had promoted sectionalism and tribalism in the past [17].

In addition to the above changes, Binaisa stated that general elections in the country would be held within two years and that they would be conducted under the UNLF umbrella, implying that no other political parties would be allowed to participate in these elections.

Binaisa's rejection of a multi-party election was based on the argument that religious and ethnic sectionalism, which had plagued Ugandan politics in the 1950s and the 1960s, would be revived. However, some leaders of the old political parties interpreted Binaisa's policy as a self-serving move intended to eliminate potential competitors for the position of the President, leaving Binaisa as the only candidate.

(iii) Binaisa's Security Policies: Binaisa's appointment as President was opposed by a number of groups. First, unlike Yusuf Lule, Binaisa was not trusted among some Baganda, for having served under Obote's government as Attorney General during the 1960s [18]. Second, within Binaisa's Cabinet itself, members of the old political parties (UPC, DP, and KY) were opposed to Binaisa's

173

policy of holding general elections under the umbrella of the UNLF. And finally, Binaisa neither had the support of nor control over the UNLF Army [19].

Faced with these challenges, Binaisa sought to consolidate his power at the centre by asserting his Presidential authority over the power brokers within the UNLF. First, he took over the key Ministry of Defense in the middle of November 1979 and demoted its former Minister, Yoweri Museveni, to the Ministry of Regional Co-operation [20]. Second, in February 1980, Binaisa demoted another strong UNLF politician, Paulo Muwanga, from the Ministry of Internal Affairs to the position of the Ugandan Ambassador to the UN in Geneva, a position that he refused to take. The NCC then forced Binaisa to take him back on the cabinet as Minister of Labour [21]. And finally, on 10 May 1980, President Binaisa made a very delicate attempt to dismiss Brigadier David Oyite-Ojok from his position of Chief of Staff of the UNLA [22]. The Military Council, under the chairmanship of Paulo Muwanga, reacted by taking over political power and putting Binaisa under indefinite house arrest [23].

Thus, within the first year following the overthrow of Amin's rule, the struggle for power among the exiles, which constituted the bulk of the UNLF, became an end in itself, thereby diverting their attention from numerous problems that bedeviled the country. In a situation where the Karamajong people of north-eastern Uganda continued to die from hunger, and where shortages of essential commodities as well as widespread violence continued to be reported in almost every district, legitimacy for the UNLF leaders mainly depended on their ability to provide basic goods and to restore order.

Rule by the Military Commission

The assumption of power in Uganda by the Military Commission on 11 May 1980 was hardly surprising, given the fact that the immediate post-Amin leaders failed not only to restore order but also to establish their legitimacy. This assumption of power by the Military Commission, however, marked yet another epoch in post-Amin politics in Uganda. First, after making a futile attempt to stop the coup, the top leadership of the NCC, including the Chairman and the Secretary -- Edward Rugumayo and Omwony Ojok, respectively -- went into exile in Kenya. Second, the Military Council reversed earlier decisions made by Binaisa's leadership regarding national elections. Elections were to be held not within two years but by December of 1980, and any number of political parties would be allowed to participate. And finally, Milton Obote returned to Uganda from his 9 years of exile in Tanzania on 27 May

1980, 16 days after the Military Commission had taken over political power in Uganda, and announced his intention to reorganize his UPC political party for the forthcoming national elections.

The 1980 National Elections in Uganda

Between May and December 1980, virtually the sole focus of government policy was the forthcoming elections, the first one to be held since Uganda's independence. The economy continued to decline and the security situation in the country worsened since, among other things, the Ugandan Liberation Army together with some Tanzanian troops still in Uganda were themselves deeply involved in armed robberies and other acts of violence [24].

By the end of June 1980, four political parties had already announced their intention to contest the forthcoming national elections. An attempt will be made below to discuss the strengths and weaknesses of each of these political parties.

(i) **The Conservative Party (CP):** Led by a former prime minister of Buganda Kingdom, Mayanja-Nkangi, this party was the weakest of the four contesting parties. Its campaign appeal was primarily based on the decentralization of power in Uganda, with strong emphasis on the restoration of former Kingdoms.

Initially, the CP sought to win political support within former Kingdoms, especially Buganda. However, realizing that voting for the CP would weaken the Democratic Party (DP), which was the main challenger to Obote's Uganda Peoples Congress (UPC), the party that the Baganda disliked most, the majority of Baganda rejected the CP and joined the DP. The CP was only supported by a handful of die-hard Baganda traditionalists whose votes were not sufficient to enable the party to win even a single seat in Parliament.

(ii) **The Uganda Patriotic Movement (UPM):** Formed on 14 June 1980 under the leadership of Yoweri Museveni, the UPM attracted strong support from the educated young and those old politicians who were exasperated by the DP-UPC feuding of the 1960s. Its campaign appeal was mainly based on ending corruption in the high echelons of government and on restoring the rule of law. Being a brand new party, having been formed within less than six months of elections, the UPM did not have enough time or money to solicit grass root support. Its support was mainly in urban areas where the educated elites lived, with the result that it could not raise

177

enough candidates to contest all the constituencies across the country. Because of these and other related problems that the UPM faced as a new party, its electoral success was limited: it managed to have only one MP elected.

(iii) The Democratic Party (DP): Led by Paul Semogerere, the DP had two advantages over all other parties: (a) being the only credible challenger to Obote's UPC, it was supported by most anti-Obote elements especially in Buganda; and (b) its old Catholic connections made it a force to reckon with at the national level. However, the DP had three major weaknesses. First, there were splits within the ranks of the party over the top leadership, some supporting the return of Yusuf Lule as the party's president and others supporting Semogerere. Second, after settling the party split over leadership in favor of Semogerere, there was yet another split between Semogerere and the party Secretary, Francis Bwengye, over ballot boxes. Semogerere supported the decision by the Military Commission that each contending party would have its separate ballot box, while Bwengye reiterated that the DP would boycott elections unless one ballot box was used for all parties in every constituency [25]. And finally, the DP did not have any military backing within the UNLA which, as I will indicate below, worked in favor of the UPC. According to the final election results,

178

the DP won 51 of the 126 seats in Parliament thus forming the main opposition party to Obote's ruling UPC.

(iv) The Uganda Peoples Congress (UPC): Led by former President Milton Obote, the UPC had a network of support across the country with the obvious exception of Buganda. Basing its campaign essentially on an appeal for reconciliation, the UPC had several advantages over other parties. First, it was decisively backed by the top leadership of the ruling Military Commission as well as by the part of the UNLA that supported the Army Chief of Staff, Brigadier David Oyite-Ojok. Second, the UPC had the money and vehicles to run an effective campaign, part of which were provided by the state and the other part by two rich Asian Ugandans, Shafiq Arain and Surdial Singh, who flew into Kampala to attend a three-day UPC delegates' conference in November 1980. And finally, led by an experienced politician, the organization of the UPC election campaign was far superior to those of other parties.

However, the UPC had its own particular problems. First, there was widespread anti-Obote feeling especially in Buganda, which led some UPC supporters to believe that the party would have done far better with a neutral leader rather than Obote. Second, most of the young educated elites that would have supported the UPC under any leadership other than that of Obote, joined the newly created UPM party. Third, having been the only party that had previously been in power for a long time, the UPC's past record of having failed to call national elections throughout its ten years in power and its use of the military force to subdue its opponents in the 1960s, were both still fresh in people's minds. And finally, some of the former strong UPC politicians (such as Mathias Ngobi, Adoko Nekyon, and Mukombe Mpambara) had switched to the DP, taking with them some of their former political supporters. Despite these and other related problems that faced the UPC, it won 72 of the 126 parliamentary seats, albeit accusations of massive rigging, and thus formed the first post-Amin elected government in Uganda [26].

However, a lot of irregularities related to the 1980 national elections in Uganda can be identified. First, prior to the elections, all contesting political parties other than the UPC had opposed the system of having separate ballot boxes in every constituency, arguing that it would allow for the easy manipulation of results. However, in support of Obote's view, Paulo Muwanga rejected the idea of having one ballot box for all candidates in every constituency in favor of one box for each candidate.

Second, the demarcation of electoral constituencies seems to have favored the UPC by giving the anti-UPC Baganda proportionately lower representation than the pro-UPC northern part of the country.

Third, 17 out of 72 seats won by the UPC were returned unopposed, including those constituencies in which candidates for other parties were either intimidated by the military or arbitrarily disqualified by the top leadership of the Military Commission.

Fourth, although the Commonwealth Observer Group approved the election results, stating that they were reasonably fair given the poor conditions under which the election was held, the decree by Paulo Muwanga on the election day that all election results had to be cleared by him before they were announced, and that failure to do so would result in a fine of half a million Ugandan shillings or a jail term of up to five years, give credence to the charge that Muwanga manipulated a lot of election results before they were publicly announced on Radio Uganda [27].

And finally, the fact that Paulo Muwanga was made the Vice-President and Minister of Defence in Obote's Cabinet, although he was not an elected member of Parliament, demonstrated at least

181

one point: that Obote rewarded Muwanga for whatever the latter had done to promote the UPC's electoral victory.

Obote's Second Term of Office (1980- 1985)

Following his return to power in December 1980, Obote decided to take over the Ministry of Finance together with his regular presidential responsibilities. Obote seems to have believed that he could easily acquire popular legitimacy for his second leadership if he rehabilitated the country's economy, a task that both Lule and Binaisa had failed to accomplish. Hence most of Obote's energies were directed towards the reconstruction of Uganda's economy, and it is to his economic policies that I will first turn.

(i) Obote's Economic Policies: Within three months of coming to office, President Obote introduced a policy statement in Parliament in which he emphasized the following as the government's guiding principles towards the country's economic recovery:(a) to raise the level of production by channeling most of the available funds to productive sectors; (b) to ensure efficiency in the productive sector and in the provision of social services; (c) to eliminate wasteful expenditure in government institutions, departments, co-operatives and parastatal organizations; (d) to ensure prudent use of funds

182

received in the form of grants and loans; (e) to promote friendship and co-operation between Uganda and donor countries and organizations; (f) to create opportunities and incentives for Ugandans and foreign private investors; and (g) to establish a mixed economy in which the state, the private sector and the co-operative movement would all play a role [28].

This economic policy contrasted sharply with Obote's economic policies in the late 1960s and early 1970s in the sense that the radicalism that had colored the latter was conspicuously missing. In particular, the new emphasis on a mixed economy as well as on the government's effort to create opportunities and incentives for private investors, contrasted sharply with Obote's pronouncement on 1 May 1970 (the Labor Day speech) in which he had sought to partially nationalize all major privately-own enterprises in Uganda, as was discussed in chapter five of this study.

Obote's departure from the economic policies of his first regime was also reflected in his first budget speech to Parliament on 1 June 1981 [29], as well as in his other policy statements [30]. In all of these the emphasis was on the recovery of the country's economy by encouraging the development of a strong private economic sector and the government's optimum utilization of foreign grants and loans, as had been recommended in part by major international donors, especially the International Monetary Fund.

Considering the fact that the Ugandan economy which Obote's second regime inherited in 1980 had been shattered by Amin's regime in the 1970s, the former's economic policies greatly improved economic conditions in the country during the early 1980s, at least in comparison with the immediately preceding years. The Gross Domestic Product (GDP) grew by 3.9 percent in 1981, the first positive economic growth since 1977; and growths in the subsequent two years (1982 and 1983) were 6.1 and 5.3 percent, respectively. As well, the annual inflation rate was reduced from 104 percent in 1980 to 30 percent in 1983 [31]. And to promote incentives among public servants and peasants, President Obote increased the former's pay by 50 percent and raised prices for cash crops grown by peasants by 33.3 percent for coffee, 20 percent for cotton, 66.5 percent for tea, 30 percent for tobacco, and 100 percent for cocoa [32].

Despite this progress towards economic recovery, Obote's leadership failed to attract much of the badly needed foreign investment. At least three related factors, arising from Obote's leadership style, seem to have been largely responsible. First,

184

some foreign investors were not sure that Obote would not resume his earlier socialist-oriented economic policies after the Ugandan economy had recovered from Amin's disastrous legacy. Second, Obote's second return to power provoked opposition among a number of subgroups in Uganda which, in the judgment of some potential private investors, made his leadership tenuous and hence non-conducive to long-term investments. And finally and most importantly, Obote's failure to improve the security situation in the country frightened many potential foreign investors. It is to the discussion of the last two factors mentioned above that I will now turn.

(ii) Obote's Administrative and Security Policies: Obote's return to power in December 1980 was resented by at least four subgroups: (a) his traditional enemies, the Baganda, who denied Obote's UPC even a single Parliamentary seat in the entire region of Buganda during the 1980 elections; (b) the other political parties which had contested the 1980 elections, especially the UPM, which believed that Obote's UPC had rigged the elections, and on the basis of that belief started waging a guerrilla war against Obote's regime [33]; (c) supporters of former Ugandan leaders (Amin, Lule, and Binaisa), who charged that Obote had rigged his way back to power, and subsequently formed their individual

185

military forces that they used to wage guerrilla war against Obote's regime; and (d) the widespread resentment in the south against the northern-dominated UNLA which caused violence in the country for which Obote's regime took the blame [34].

All this opposition to Obote's leadership not only created problems of legitimacy for his regime, but also led to other constraints on establishing a system of order in Uganda, as will be indicated below.

(iii) Human Rights Violations: Within the first year of Obote's second term of office, there were so many arbitrary arrests and killings in Uganda as to attract the serious concern of Amnesty International, whose officials visited Uganda in January 1982 and then later made several representations to Obote's government to reduce its alarming record of human rights violations [35]. Despite these representations, such violations continued to increase so much that by the time Obote's regime was removed in a coup on 27 July 1985, it was held responsible for the deaths of more than 300,000 civilians [36].

Besides these killings, thousands of people were made homeless during Obote's second leadership. The government's suspicion that refugees who had fled from Rwanda to south-western Uganda in the early 1960s would be recruited by Museveni into his guerrilla force against his regime, led Obote to drive those refugees out of their homes. Subsequently, about 25,000 of them crossed back to Rwanda from where they had originally fled [37].

Moreover, more than 50,000 Ugandans were forced by the government to leave their homes in the so-called "Luwero triangle" on two grounds: (a) that inhabitants of this area were being recruited into guerrilla forces; and (b) that in order for government troops to carry out counter-operations against guerrilla forces believed to be in the area, civilians had to be evacuated. The tragedy, however, was that thousands of inhabitants were killed by government troops who had been given powers to shoot to kill on sight any suspected guerrillas [38]. The rest were forced to live in concentration camps organized by the government.

(iv) Guerrilla Wars: At least three main guerrilla forces launched persistent military attacks against Obote's regime during the period 1980-1985: a force, the strongest of the three, headed by Yoweri Museveni (former Minister of Defence in both Lule's and Binaisa's regimes); a force led by Andrew Kayiira (former Minister of Internal

Affairs in Lule's government; and a force under the leadership of Moses Ali (former Minister of Finance in Amin's rule) [39].

As a counter-force to these guerrilla armies, Obote formed a personal security force, the National Security Agency (NASA), in addition to the regular Ugandan National Liberation Army (UNLA), both of which were characterized by a high level of indiscipline and poor training. During constant armed conflicts between Obote's security forces and guerrilla armies, innocent civilians suffered most.

But Obote's ill-trained and undisciplined security forces not only fought wars against guerrilla armies, they also became involved in committing crimes, including armed robberies, harassment of civilians, looting, rape and many other forms of violence against Ugandan society as a whole. Obote's failure to discipline and control his security forces seriously undermined his aspiration to acquire popular legitimacy for his regime. Just one month before his regime was overthrown by the army, Amnesty International reported widespread and systematic torture and murder of civilians by security forces, and accused Obote of failure to take corrective action [40]. Part of the explanation for Obote's failure to control his security forces lay in serious divisions within the ranks of his government, to which I will now turn.

(v) **Factionalism within the Government:** Within less than four months after Obote had been restored to power for the second time, his cabinet was rife with factionalism: the main axis was between President Obote himself and his Vice-President, Paulo Muwanga. The conflict between these two came to a head when Obote sought to appoint his cousin and former head of his personal security force (the General Service Unit) in the late 1960s and early 1970s -- Akena Adoko -- as the chairman of the Public Service Commission. Vice-President Muwanga, who was also the Minister of Defence, was so strongly opposed to this appointment that he threatened to resign from the Cabinet altogether if it was carried through [41]. Although Obote ultimately cancelled this appointment, conflicts between him and Muwanga never ceased until Obote was removed from power in July 1985, through a military coup that Muwanga supported [42].

More serious than the conflict between Obote and his Vice-President, was the high degree of factionalism within Obote's security forces, and more particularly within the Army (the UNLA). The struggle for control was between old allies -- the Acholi and

Langi soldiers - who together had hitherto dominated the Ugandan military since independence, except during Amin's rule when they were both purged on the grounds that they had supported, and benefited from, Obote's first regime.

The split between the Langi and Acholi first became visible in August 1981, when a plot to assassinate President Obote in the Acholi town of Kitgum was unearthed. Following this incident, the Acholi military commander of Buganda region, Lt. Colonel Basilio Olara Okello, was forced to move his headquarters from Kampala to Bombo, 15 miles to the north of the capital, and Lt. Colonel Francis Olwo (a Langi) was put in charge of Kampala [43]. Hardly a month later, a typed document listing the Acholi grievances against the Langi was distributed throughout Kampala. Included among these grievances was a charge that Obote's leadership discriminated against the Acholi in both new appointments and promotions, especially within the UNLA [44]. In late December 1981, Lt. Colonel Peter Odoma (one of the leading Acholi soldiers) was arrested and detained, having been accused of plotting to overthrow Obote's government through a military coup. Whether or not this accusation was valid, an armed conflict between Langi and Acholi soldiers was reported on December 21 and 22, a period during which Peter Odoma was arrested [45].

To fuel the growing antagonism between these two factions within the army, President Obote promoted his fellow Langi, Lt. Colonel Smith Opon-Acak, to the position of Brigadier, and subsequently made him the Army Chief of Staff in August 1984, to replace another Langi (the late Major General David Oyite-Ojok) who had died in a mysterious helicopter crash on 2 December 1983 [46].

The appointment of Opon-Acak aggrieved Acholi soldiers for at least three main reasons. First, the only senior Acholi Military Officer, General Tito Okello, had already reached retirement age, being 71 years old, and his retirement would leave no Acholi in any key military position. Second, among the front-runners for the position of Army Chief of Staff, following the death of Oyite-Ojok, was Basilio Okello, an Acholi Lieutenant Colonel who was senior to Opon-Acak. And finally, Acholi soldiers later accused the new Army Chief of Staff (Opon-Acak) not only of favoring his fellow Langi soldiers in both promotions and new appointments, but also of ordering only Acholi soldiers to go and fight against guerrilla armies while their Langi colleagues stayed behind [47].

The Acholis' dissatisfaction with Obote's leadership prompted them to make secret contacts with leaders of guerrilla armies to gain some cooperation for their plot to overthrow the government. Such a secret meeting was arranged in Kampala in October 1984 between a senior NRA representative (the late Lt. Sam Katabarwa) and three leading Acholi figures -- General Tito Okello, Lt. Colonel Basilio Okello, and the then Prime Minister Otema Alimadi -- as well as Vice-President Paulo Muwanga [48].

Similar meetings are believed to have been held with Amin's former soldiers who were carrying out guerrilla activities in northern Uganda, as was later reflected by their active participation, along with Acholi soldiers, in the military coup of 27 July 1985. Moreover, having made contacts with leaders of guerrilla forces, Acholi soldiers began to disobey orders issued by the new Army Chief of Staff, requiring them to embark on offensive wars against guerrillas [49]. Then, on 7 July 1985, a fight between the Langi and Acholi soldiers over weapons took place at Mbuya barracks, during which at least 30 people were killed [50].

Following this incident, the Army commander, Tito Okello, together with Lt. Colonel Basilio Okello left for the main Acholi town of Gulu where they prepared their troops for a final showdown. With the help of some of Amin's former soldiers, the Acholi troops defeated the Langi force commanded by Opon-Acak at Karuma Falls on 26

July 1985. The following morning Kampala fell, and Milton Obote was once again forced into a second exile, this time in Zambia.

It appears thus far that the levels of political disorder during Obote's second regime were at par with those of Amin's regime, discussed in chapter six. First, the record of human rights violations in both regimes was particularly alarming. Second, both Amin and Obote fashioned their personal security forces, recruited largely from their respective ethnic groups, on which they individually depended for their own political survival. Third, neither Obote nor Amin was able to control excesses committed by their respective security forces, which in both cases were highly undisciplined, fragmented, and ill-trained. Fourth, although for different reasons, both Amin and Obote expelled foreign minority groups from Uganda -- Asians in 1972 and Rwandese in 1982, respectively, and usurped their properties. Fifth, both regimes provoked the emergence of guerrilla forces that subsequently played a vital role in their eventual removal from power. And finally, both regimes were characterized by high levels of factionalism within the ranks of government structures and by a rule of terror. In all essentials, therefore, Obote's second regime, like that of Amin, was based primarily on dictatorial rule.

Tito Okello's Regime (July 27 1985- January 1986)

Following the successful coup on 27 July 1985, a nine man Military Council to govern the country was announced. The Council was headed by Major General Tito Okello, former Military Commander of the UNLA, who was also made the head of state. Other members of the Council included: Brigadier Basilio Okello, who had led the military coup and who subsequently became the new Army Commander; Colonel Wilson Toko, former General Manager of Uganda Airways, who subsequently became the Vice-Chairman of the Military Council and Minister of Defence; Colonel Zedi Maruru, who had announced the coup over Radio Uganda; Lieutenant Colonel Nanyumba; Colonel Fred Oketcho; Colonel Jack Nyero; Justin Okot, a lawyer who was made the Secretary to the Council; and Salim Saleh, the only NRA representative on the Council who declined the offer on the ground that the NRA was inadequately represented on the Council [55].

Although the Acholi soldiers had removed Obote from power on the accusation that he had favored soldiers from his ethnic group in both promotions and new appointments, five of the nine members of the newly established ruling Military Council were themselves from Acholi. This blatant failure, on the part of the Acholi soldiers, to avoid similar mistakes on the basis of which they had removed Obote from power, ultimately led to their own downfall. For, as will be indicated below, Museveni's NRA sought to acquire parity with these new leaders, leading to a major struggle for power during which the Acholi soldiers were forcibly removed from office in late January 1986.

(i) Power Struggle between the UNLA and NRA: In the wake of the 1985 coup, the NRA guerrillas demanded that:(a) half the members of the ruling Military Council should be replaced by NRA representatives; and (b) no formal government other than the interim Military Council, should be established. The new rulers, however, disregarded NRA's demands and appointed Paulo Muwanga as an executive Prime Minister, charged with the responsibility of forming a cabinet that would be answerable to the Military Council. The NRA retaliated by resuming offensive attacks against the new regime, thereby disrupting an informal cease fire that had been in effect for about a month since the coup. In gestures of conciliation to the NRA, Paulo Muwanga was dismissed as Prime Minister only three weeks after taking office, and peace talks between military rulers and the NRA were initiated in neighboring Kenya on 26 August 1985 [52].

195

(ii) The Nairobi Peace Negotiations: Peace negotiations between UNLA and NRA delegations, which were chaired by President arap Moi of Kenya, began on 26 August and ended on 17 December 1985. These talks, however, were characterized by nagging differences between the main protagonists in the struggle for power, and hence involved several adjournments for consultation on a number of issues.

Among the many areas of disagreement between the two parties [53], at least four main ones can be identified which, put together, indicate further the extent to which both competition and conflicts among political elites in Uganda have continued to be a major source of disorder in that country.

The first disagreement was over representation on the Military Council. Initially, Museveni refused to recognize Major General Tito Okello as head of state, considering him instead as a leader of an army like Museveni himself. Museveni's NRA, moreover, refused to recognize the military government which they regarded as a mere change of guard from the Obote regime which the NRA had been fighting since 1981. On the basis of these contentions, the NRA delegation to the peace talks in Nairobi proposed that both Okello's and Museveni's military forces should be equally represented on

196

the ruling Military Council, and that other members of this Council should be representatives of the four political parties that had participated in the 1980 elections. The UNLA delegation, on the other hand, insisted that other smaller military forces, including: the Uganda Freedom Movement, the Uganda National Rescue Front, the Federal Democratic Movement, and the former Uganda National Army should be given representation on the Council.

This disagreement was eventually settled as follows: (a) both the UNLA and NRA were each to have seven seats on the Military Council although Tito Okello, who was to remain the Chairman of the Council and head of state, was not included among the UNLA numbers; (b) other smaller military forces were to have a seat each, except the Federal Democratic Movement which was allowed two seats; and (c) the Military Council thus constituted was to consult the four political parties that participated in the 1980 elections, with a view to deciding the mode of their representation on the Council [54].

The second was over the position of the Vice-Chairman of the Military Council. The NRA delegation insisted that the position of the Vice-Chairman of the Military Council should be taken by Yoweri Museveni. Since the then Vice-Chairman, Colonel Wilson Toko, was also the leader of the UNLA delegation during the

Nairobi peace negotiations, this demand by the NRA provided another area of disagreement. However, it was finally resolved that the leader of the NRA should be the Vice-Chairman of the Council, and that in the absence of the Chairman the former should exercise the powers and perform the duties and functions of head of state [55].

The third area of disagreement was related to the composition of the new national army. Both the UNLA and the NRA were cautious about being outnumbered by the other side. The distribution in the final agreement was as follows: the UNLA was to have 3,700 soldiers, the NRA 3,580, and the other smaller forces 1,200, making a total of 8,480 soldiers. It was also stressed that the new national army thus constituted should be broad-based and representative of the whole country [56].

The fourth was over persons who served in Amin's regime. The NRA delegation resented the UNLA's proposal that soldiers who served in Amin's regime should be represented on the Military Council, let alone recruited into the new national army. The NRA's resentment was based on the view that those soldiers were mainly responsible for most of social ills with which Uganda had been afflicted since Amin's dictatorship.

198

The UNLA delegation, on the other hand, argued that: (a) the spirit of national reconciliation could not be based on vengeance; and (b) the NRA resented ex-Amin soldiers primarily because most of them came from northern Uganda unlike the southern-oriented NRA forces. It was eventually agreed that: (i) all persons who had committed atrocities and other crimes, both during and after Amin's regime, should be punished according to law; (ii) all persons who had served in Amin's notorious State Research Bureau and Public Safety Unit should not be eligible to join any security force in Uganda; and (iii) all ex-soldiers who had served in the army during the period 1971-1979 and who were not covered under (i) above, should be carefully screened before they were admitted to the new national army, and that preference should be given to those with special skills to fill places which could not otherwise be filled [57].

In addition to the above areas of agreement between the two protagonists in the struggle for power, other important general agreements were made during the Nairobi peace talks. First, it was agreed that observer forces should be invited from four Commonwealth countries -- Kenya, Tanzania, Britain and Canada -- to monitor the cease fire and to assist in the recruitment and training of the new national army. Second, it was agreed that during its first meeting, the newly constituted Military Council should discuss and resolve matters relating to the following issues: (i) review of all decrees promulgated by Okello's government since 27 July 1985; (ii) formulation of broad guidelines for the government program of action; (iii) establishment and formulation of the terms of reference for a commission of inquiry into the violation of human rights in Uganda since independence; (iv) formulation of guidelines for reconstructing the national army and strategies for the rehabilitation of soldiers who would not be recruited into the new army; and (v) review of cabinet portfolios and other political appointments by Okello's military government since 27 July 1985 [58]. In the remaining part of this chapter, I will evaluate the peace agreement discussed above.

(iii) Evaluation of the Peace Agreement: Although the final draft of the Nairobi peace agreement looked good on paper, chances for its implementation were negligible. There were a number of problems that could hardly be resolved by this formal agreement and which were sufficiently salient to wreck its implementation. As well, some aspects of this agreement were detrimental to its implementation. It is to the discussion of a combination of these problems that I will now turn.

First, the animosity displayed between the UNLA and the NRA both before and even during the period when peace negotiations were underway in Nairobi minimized chances for reconciliation. When Okello coup took place, the NRA had already reached close to Kampala and was thus angry at the UNLA for having hijacked its revolution for which it had fought since 1981. The NRA also discredited the UNLA for its continued gross indiscipline even after the coup of 27 July 1985. Hence, it was unrealistic to assume that these highly antagonistic forces could be integrated to form a cohesive national army following the signing of the Nairobi peace agreement.

Second, when Museveni went into the bush to wage a guerrilla war against Obote's second regime, his intentions were to overthrow the regime and to take over the government. Similarly, underlying the Acholis' urge to overthrow Obote's regime was the desire to take over the instruments of government on the basis of which they could acquire what Obote had deprived them of: power, prestige and wealth. After the common enemy (Obote's regime) had been removed, there was a struggle for ultimate power between the Acholi soldiers and the NRA, which was directly exposed during the peace negotiations in Nairobi. In view of what transpired in the wake of the Nairobi peace agreement, it became clear that the entire process of peace negotiations had been mere window dressing. Within a few days of the signing of this agreement, there was a renewed armed conflict between the UNLA and NRA, each accusing the other of violating the agreement [59].

Third, the Nairobi peace negotiations excluded the participation of representative political groups such as political parties and any other organizations that were representative of the people. Lacking such input, it remained to be seen whether a peace agreement made between two rival armies, each of which had its own interests to protect, could last.

Fourth, Article 17(c) of the agreement called for the establishment of a commission of inquiry into the violation of human rights in Uganda since independence. Genuine as this clause of the agreement was, it seems to have threatened the very foundation of the UNLA, since a large number within its ranks including some top military leaders themselves, could have been implicated if such a commission was set up and functioned.

Fifth, article 7 of the agreement provided for the establishment of a small nucleus national army, composed of only 8,480 soldiers. For the UNLA, whose troop size at the time numbered no less than

15,000, the small size of the new army signaled a bleak future for employment. This sense of insecurity within the ranks of the UNLA led to two main adverse effects: (i) a rift developed within the existing Military Council where some of its members felt that President Tito Okello had conceded too much to the NRA; and (ii) some UNLA troops decided to go on a looting spree in and around Kampala, during which more than 300 civilians were reported killed. And in the attempt to conceal these atrocities the then Army Commander, Brigadier Basilio Okello, banned news reporters from publishing any more news items on his security forces [60].

And finally, following the signing of the peace agreement, the NRA troops became more determined than ever before to drive out Okello's military government and to take over all the power. At least three main factors seem to have helped the NRA to attain its ambition. First, following the 27 July coup, which toppled Obote, the UNLA was weakened. Langi soldiers who together with Acholi soldiers had earlier constituted the backbone of the UNLA, had either fled the country or been killed during the coup. Second, the UNLA troops were not as well trained as NRA troops. This lack of training, coupled with their low level of discipline, made the UNLA troops less committed to withstand the NRA's assault. And finally, the NRA's morale was boosted by popular support from civilians who were disillusioned with the UNLA's lack of discipline. With all these factors in their favor, the NRA's troops began their final assault on 17 January 1986 and by 29th of the same month Kampala had fallen to the NRA and Museveni was sworn in as the new President of Uganda [61].

CONCLUSION

As the preceding discussion has indicated, post-Amin regimes in Uganda not only failed to establish the supremacy of civil political institutions over the military, but they also failed either to acquire popular legitimacy or to restore political order in a country that had been ravaged by Amin's eight years of arbitrary dictatorial rule.

Rather than seeking to re-establish their legitimacy, the first two post-Amin regimes in Uganda were primarily preoccupied with the question "who gets what?" Both Lule and Binaisa were charged with corruption, first, in relation to the distribution of property and businesses abandoned by the flight of Amin's supporters, and second, in appointing their close associates to key political positions. Even more crucial, neither Lule nor Binaisa made a serious effort to restore order or to provide a degree of security in the country.

Even worse than either Lule's or Binaisa's regime was Obote's second leadership which, lacking popular legitimacy, decided to depend on highly undisciplined security forces to enforce public compliance. Instead of disciplining his military, Obote used it as a force of repression against his political opponents, at the same time that he exacerbated factionalism within it by providing preferential treatment to soldiers from his own ethnic group. In other words, the conditions that had originally fostered military intervention against Obote's first regime in the early 1970s, discussed in chapter five, were even more prevalent in his second regime in the 1980s, leading ultimately to his second overthrow.

What has perplexed both scholars and observers of Obote's politics has been his tendency to repeat similar mistakes that had previously led to the downfall of his first leadership, as if he never learnt anything during his nine years of exile in Tanzania. Even more distressing is the general failure of Ugandan political leaders to learn from each other's mistakes.

In particular, post-Amin leaders repeated each other's mistakes: both corruption and factionalism characterized their politics, and none of them was able either to restore order and internal security or to acquire any measure of popular legitimacy. Unfortunately, such mistakes were not unique to post-Amin leadership. As indicated in early chapters of this study, colonial leadership was imposed upon Ugandans, most of who never recognized it as legitimate. Moreover, Obote's first regime and that of Amin were both characterized by factional politics, lack of popular legitimacy, and political instability.

206

NOTES

[1] For a detailed account on this meeting see especially Omara Atuba, <u>The Uganda National Liberation Front, The Gospel of Liberation</u>, Moshi, Tanzania, 1979. This meeting attracted most Ugandan exile groups from all over the World, and at least twenty-eight of such groups were represented.

[2] Edward Rugumayo, leader of one of Lusaka groups, was elected the chairman of the NCC and Rex Omwony Ojok, of the Dar as Salaam group, was elected the NCC Secretary.

[3] Problems arising from Amin's legacy are discussed in some detail in <u>The Rehabilitation of the Economy of Uganda: A Report by a Commonwealth Team of Experts (The Seers Report)</u>, London, Commonwealth Secretariat, June 1979.

[4] For a full list of Lule's cabinet, see <u>Africa Research Bulletin: Political, Social and Cultural Series</u>, 16 May 1979.

[5] <u>The Seers Report</u>, paragraph 62.

[6] Africa Research Bulletin: Political, Social and Cultural Series, 15 July, 1979, pp.5297-5301.

[7] Africa Research Bulletin: Political, Social and Cultural Series, 15 June, 1979, pp.5261-5262.

[8] Weekly Review, 29 June 1979, pp.5-13. These fears were strengthened by Lule's re-establishment of the four pre-Amin provinces of which Buganda was the most densely populated.

[9] See Africa Confidential, 15 April 1979, pp. 4-7. It is important to note, however, that these ideological divisions were cross-cutting rather than reinforcing regional and ethnic divisions. While Lule came from southern Uganda, Martin Aliker who was his chief advisor came from northern Uganda. As well, Obote's strongest supporter in Lule's cabinet, Paulo Muwang, came from Buganda.

[10] Africa Confidential, 20 June 1979, pp. 2-4.

[11] Africa Research Bulletin: Political, Social and Cultural Series, 6 July 1979, P.5298.

[12] Ibid., P.5299.

[13] Gertzel, "Uganda After Amin", p.461.

[14] For a full list of Binaisa's Cabinet, See Africa Research Bulletin: Political, Social and Cultural Series, 16 July 1979.

[15] See Uganda Times, 19 October 1979.

[16] Africa Research Bulletin: Political, Social and Cultural Series, 16 November 1979, P.5440.

[17] This accusation was made by Paul Semogerere, former Publicity Secretary of the DP in 1960s and Minister of Labour on Binaisa's Cabinet. See Weekly Review, 14 September 1979.

[18] Weekly Review, 17 August 1979.

[19] Africa Research Bulletin: Political, Social and Cultural Series, 16 October 1979, pp.5413-5414.

[20] There were three major factions in the Ugandan National Liberation Army (UNLA) at the time: (i) soldiers who supported Yoweri Museveni (Minister of Defence) who were mainly drawn from western Uganda, and more particularly from Ankole district which is Museveni's home area; (ii) soldiers who supported Oyite-

Ojok (Army Chief of Staff), mainly from the latter's district of Lango; and (iii) other soldiers who supported Tito Okello (Army Commander), the majority of whom came from Okello's district of Acholi. See Africa Confidential, 22 August 1979, P.4.

[21] See Africa Confidential, 28 November 1979, pp.5-6.

[22] Africa Research Bulletin: Political, Social and Cultural Series, 17 March 1980, P.5585.

[23] Africa Confidential, 4 June 1980, pp.6-8.

[24] Africa Research Bulletin: Political, Social and Cultural Series, 17 June 1980,pp.5682-5686. The Military Commission which took over power was composed as follows: Paulo Muwanga (Chairman), Yoweri Museveni (Vice-Chairman), Brigadier David Oyit-Ojok, Major General Tito Okello, Colonel Zeddi Maruru, and Lt. Colonel William Omaria.

[25] Part of the explanation for the army involvement in acts of violence is that many soldiers were recrutied without being included on the pay roll. Yet they were given uniforms and guns. Moreover, the Tanzanian troops were gradually becoming regarded by most

Ugandans as an army of occupation rather than of liberation, and some of them decided to seek means of enriching themselves before they were withdrawn from Uganda.

[26] Ultimately DP members supported Semogerere, fearing that the boycott of elections would lead to UPC's victory without any opposition. Consequently, Francis Bwengye resigned from being the Secretary of the party and went into exile in Kenya.

[27] For a detailed official account of electoral results, see Report of the Electoral Commission 1980: Presented to His Excellency Dr. A. Milton Obote MP, President of the Republic of Uganda, Entebbe, Government Printer, 25 June 1981, pp.92-189.

[28] For some of these charges, See Africa Confidential, 11 February 1981, pp.1-3.

[29] A.Milton Obote, Communication From the Chair: The Challenge of Recovery, Entebbe, Government Printer, 17 March 1981.

[30] A. Milton Obote, Budget Speech: First Step to Recovery, Entebbe, Government Printer, June 1981.

[31] These documents included: Budget Speech: Programme for Recovery, Entebbe, Government Printer, June 1982; Communication From the Chair: Progress to Recovery, Entebbe, Government Printer, March 1982; Communication from the Chair: Platform for Recovery, Entebbe, Government Printer, March 1983; and Revised Recovery Programme, Entebbe, Government Printer, September 1983.

[32] See Jane Carroll, "Uganda: Recent Economy", in Africa South of the Sahara, 1986, 15th Edition, London, Europa Publications, 1986, p.966. For a detailed coverage of these statistics and others dealing with the improvement of Uganda's economy during Obote's second term of office, see Ministry of Planning and Economic Development, Background to the Budget 1984-1985, Entebbe, Government Printer, June 1984.

[33] Milton Obote, Budget Speech: Climbing to Recovery, Entebbe, Government printer, June 1983.

[34] See especially Africa Research Bulletin: Political, Social and Cultural Series,18 March 1981, pp.5970-5972; and 18 April 1981, pp.5998-5999.

[35] Africa Research Bulletin: Political, Social and Cultural Series, 18 June 1981, P.6051; and 18 November 1981, pp.6256-6257. Though not very cohesive, these groups resorted to persistent guerrilla activities and/or sabotage as the means of removing Obote from power.

[36] See Memorandum to the Government of Uganda on an Amnesty International Mission to Uganada in January 1982 and Further Exchanges between the Government and Amnesty International, London, Amnesty International Secretariat, April 1983.

[37] This was an estimate provided by Amnesty International. See Africa Research Bulletin: Political Series, 15 September 1985, p.7761.

[38] See Africa Research Bulletin: Political, Social and Cultural Series, 19 Ocotober 1982, pp.6613-6614.

[39] Africa Confidential, 8 June 1983, pp.3-7; and 15 August 1984, pp1-3.

[40] Museveni's force, the National Resistance Army (NRA), mainly operated in western Uganda. Kayiira's Uganda Freedom Army (UFA) operated mainly in Buganda. Moses Ali's Uganda National Rescue Front (UNRF) operated mainly in northern Uganda.

[41] See Africa South of the Sahara, 1986, 15th edition, London, Europa Publication, Richard Walker, "Uganda: Recent History", in 1986, p.991; Africa Research Bulletin: Political, Social and Cultural Series, 15 June 1985, P. 7659; and 15 July 1985, p.7689.

[42] Africa Confidential, 8 April 1981.

[43] As was reflected by his being appointed as the executive Prime Minister by the Military government that had overthrown Obote, Paulo Muwanga is believed to have been involved in a plot to remove Obote from power.

[44] Africa Confidential, 15 September 1981.

[45] Africa Confidential, 15 October 1981.

[45] Africa Confidential, 3 February 1982.

[46] <u>Africa Confidential</u>, 15 August 1984.

[47] See <u>Africa Research Bulletin: Political Series,</u>
15 August 1985, P.7721; and <u>Africa</u>, September 1985, P.36.

[48] Unfortunately Lt. Sam Katabarwa was intercepted by Obote's notorious National Security Agency (NASA) before he left Kampala, and despite apparent efforts by Prime Minister Otema Alimadi and Vice-President Paulo Muwanga to save his life, he was killed on the order of a Langi Military officer, Lt. Egore.

[49] Such was the case when, in June 1985, Acholi soldiers at Magamaga Ordnance depot refused to move to western Uganda to engage the NRA. When the Chief of Staff sent some Langi troops to persuade these soldiers to change their minds, an armed conflict ensued between these two groups.

[50] The weapons these factions were fighting over had been imported by the government and destined for the major Lango town of Lira in preparation for any possible military conflict between the Langi and Acholi soldiers. However, Muwanga's security officers at Entebbe airport intercepted them and redirected them to Mbuya barracks commanded by an Acholi officer. Opon-Acak sent his

fellow Langi soldiers to collect these weapons that the Acholi soldiers refused to release. See Africa Confidential, 31 August 1985, P.4.

[51] Africa Research Bulletin: Political Series, 15 August 1985, pp. 7723-7724.

[52] Africa Research Bulletin: Political Series, 15 September 1985, pp. 7760-7761.
Since Museveni doubted Tanzania's impartiality in hosting these talks, both the NRA and UNLA agreed on Kenya as the hosting country.

[53] For a detailed coverage on disagreements and conflict between Okello's Military government and Museveni's NRA between August to December 1985, from which the summary presented in this section was derived, see especially: Africa Research Bulletin: Political Series, 15 September 1985,15 October 1985, 15 November 1985, and 15 December 1985; Africa Confidential, 4 September 1985, 27 November 1985, and 11 December 1985; The Weekly Review, October 18 and 25, November 8 and 15, and December 6 and 13; and Africa, September, October and December 1985 issues.

[54] See The Uganda Peace Agreement, 17 December 1985, Article 2. This settlement together with other settlements presented in this section have been summarized by the author from The Peace Agreement, which was signed by Tito Okello and Yoweri Museveni in the presence of President arap Moi of Kenya in Nairobi on 17 December 1985. For a full text of this Peace Agreement, see The Weekly Review, 20 December 1985, pp.10-13.

[55] The Peace Agreement, Article 3.

[56] Ibid., Articles 7-8.

[57] Ibid., Article 14.

[58] Ibid., Article 17.

[59] The Weekly Review, 17 January 1986.

[60] The Weekly Review, 10 January 1986.

[61] For details of the war between the NRA and UNLA before Kampala was taken over by the former, see especially: Africa Confidential, 29 January 1986; The Weekly Review, 31 January

1986; and Africa Research Bulletin: Political Series, 15 February 1986.

CHAPTER VII

MUSEVENI'S LEADERSHIP (1986- Present)

Museveni came into power under complete different circumstances, in comparison with his predecessors. His was no palace coup nor was he elected into the office. Instead, his National Resistance Army (NRA) waged an armed struggle against the Ugandan government for five years, from February 1981 until it ultimately gained power in January 1986.

In his swearing-in address on 29 January 1986, Museveni outlined what he called "salient points" of his National Resistance Movement (NRM) leadership programme: (i) restoration of democracy, arguing that democracy "is not a favour from any government: it is the natural right of the people" [1]; (ii) provision of security to both people and their property, for, "the people of Uganda should only die from natural causes that are beyond our control, but not at the hands of fellow citizens" [2]; (iii) consolidation of national unity, devoid of religious and tribal divisions as well as divisions along political party lines [3]; and (iv) promoting regional cooperation in economic matters, especially in transport and communication within East Africa [4].

The above four salient points provided a springboard for the development later of ten points that the NRM government, led by Museveni, sought to govern the country [5]. For purposes of comparison, the current Museveni regime will be judged on its capacity to attain what other previous post-colonial regimes in Uganda failed to achieve: (i) acquiring popular legitimacy, (ii) reviving the economy, (iii) avoiding factional politics, (iv) avoiding corruption; and (v) establishing a disciplined, representative, and dependable security force.

(i) Popular Legitimacy

The cornerstone of Museveni's administrative policies has been the Resistance Council (RC) system. In fact the concept of democracy, which constitutes the first of the ten-point NRM programme, is rooted in the RC system that was established all over Uganda immediately after Museveni took over power. Below are the basics of the RC system, from 1986 up to 1997, on the basis of which Museveni's government sought to attain popular legitimacy.

At the village level (which is the lowest administrative unit in Uganda), all residents who are eligible to vote (18 years and above) constitute a village Resistance Council (RC I). Members of RC I elect from among themselves nine officials to constitute the Village Resistance Executive Committee (Chairman, Vice-Chairman, General Secretary, and Secretaries of: Women, Youth, Education, Information, Security, and Mass mobilization).

All members of Village Resistance Executive committees in a parish (the second basic administrative unit) form the Parish Resistance Council (RC II), and elect an executive committee of nine officials from among themselves. All members of parish executive committees in a sub-county form the Sub-county Resistance Council (RC III) who elect, from among themselves, the sub-county executive committee. All members of the sub-county executive committees in a county form a County Resistance Council (RC IV), which elects its executive committee from among its members.

The District Resistance Council (the apex of local government) was composed of two representatives from every sub-county council and every town council in the district, as well as one woman elected by every county council and every municipal council in the district.

The Local Government Act of 1997 made some changes. The act made a distinction between rural and urban local governments on the one hand and between local governments and local administrative units on the other [5].

Under the act, the system of the local government is based on the district as the top unit, along which there are other local governments as follows [7]: (1) Local Government in a district rural area, made up of: (i) the District Council, and (ii) the Sub-county Councils; (2) Local Government in a city, made up of: (i) the City Council, and (ii) the City Division Councils; (3) Local Government in a municipality, made up of: (i) the Municipal Council, and the Municipal Division Councils; and (4) Local Government in a town, made up of: Town Council.

Administrative units are three-fold [8]: (i) County Council, composed of members of sub-county executive committees in the county; (ii) Parish Council, composed of members of village executive committees in the Parish; and (iii) Village Council, composed of all persons of 18 years of age and over, residing in the village.

The main difference between local governments and local administrative units is that the latter are indirectly elected while the former are directly elected. Otherwise, the main objective of the Local Government Act of 1997 was to bring government, and services associated with it, closer to the people. In particular, the act sought to "ensure democratic participation and control of decision making by the people concerned" [9].

Thus, more than any previous governments in Uganda, Museveni's has made much effort in the decentralization of power, responsibilities and functions at all levels of local government. The original Resistance Council System has, therefore, provided a framework for democratic decentralization in Uganda [10].

Other aspects of democracy that have been attained by Museveni's government include: (i) freedom of expression, especially in the press; (ii) establishment of a new national constitution in 1995, based on heavy consultation with people at grass-root level; (iii) conducting a referendum in July 2000 to establish the preferred political system for Uganda; and (iv) improvements in human rights, in comparison with previous regimes.

All the above elements of democratic participation have combined to make Museveni's regime popular and legitimate, especially among the rural population, as reflected through Museveni's high-level victory in two consecutive presidential elections [11].

However, the NRM government has also been criticised as being anti-democratic for denying multi-party politics in the country. Museveni's government has led the country under the movement political system, which is held by NRM officials to be open to all Ugandans and where leaders are supposed to be chosen only on the basis of merit. Thus, the Museveni government upholds clause 24 of the political organization bill, which states in part that:

> During the period when the movement political system is in force, political activities may continue except that no political party or organization shall sponsor or offer a platform to or in anyway campaign for or against a candidate in any presidential or parliamentary elections or any other organized by the Electoral Commission.

The clause also bars political parties from using symbols, slogans, colours or names identifying any political party. Moreover, political parties are neither allowed to open offices below the national level nor to hold public meetings.

The main arguments put forward by Museveni's government for denying multi-party politics in Uganda are two-fold. First, that party politics previously divided the country along both religious and ethnic lines. And second, that the movement system is intended to

224

accommodate all Ugandans who can, therefore, compete on the basis of individual merit for electoral public office under its umbrella.

As indicated in early chapters of this study, the first argument above holds true. However, the second argument may be difficult to defend. The case in point is the last presidential elections in March 2001. When Dr. Kizza Besigye decided to run for the presidency, the National Executive Committee of the NRM did not support his candidacy. Instead, they urged Museveni to be the sole movement candidate for the presidency. Clearly, this undermined the principle of individual merit, supposed to be the corner stone of the movement system.

In early 2003, however, president Musiveni started to soften his stand on political parties, mainly due the pressure from international donors who wanted to see multiparty activity in Uganda as an element of democracy. Thus, in March 2003, the National Conference, which is the highest organ of the NRM that is chaired by president Museveni himself, adopted a resolution to open up political space for political parties.

Despite this change of heart on the part of the president, political party activists in Uganda have been openly disappointed. There are two main sources of that disappointment: (i) the condition attached to the resolution that the opening up of political space should be sanctioned through a national referendum; and (ii) the proposal by president Museveni, which was also overwhelmingly supported and adopted by the same National Conference, that the constitutional two-term limit on the presidency should be lifted [12].

(ii) The Econmy

The NRM government inherited not only empty coffers but also extensive external debt. One of its first challenges, therefore, was how to turn round that sad economic situation. Accordingly, the fifth of the NRM ten-point progamme dealt with laying the foundation for an independent, integrated and self-sustaining national economy. At least, six steps have been undertaken in the attempt to achieve these objectives.

1. Under the banner of "mixed economy", the NRM government has liberalized the economy at the same time that it has sought to diversify into non-traditional exports (such as beans, ground nuts, fish, etc) in order to avoid previous dependency on coffee and cotton for export.

2. Since its inception in 1986, Museveni's government has carried out such impressive socio-economic and political reforms that have captured positive attention of the international donor community.

3. More than any other regime in Ugandan history, Museveni's government has encouraged private business as matter of government policy, leading to a huge increase in investor's country credit rating from 7.3 in 1993 to 22.9 in 2000 [13].

4. Tax collection in Uganda has increased from Uganda shillings 44 billion in 1988 to 1,000 billion in December 2000 [14]. This increase may be partly explained by the establishment of the Revenue Authority by the government and partly by sustainable economic policies.

5. Since 1997, Museveni's government has launched universal primary education that has led to an increase in children's enrolment from 2.5 million in 1997 to 6.8 million in the year 2000 [15].

6. Since 1993, the NRM government has been involved in the process of privatising public enterprises, most of which had

previously been a drain on public purse. By June 2000, 93 public enterprises had been divested, leaving 46 others being processed for divestiture [16].

Because of the above and other related economic successes, Uganda currently enjoys unprecedented favourable international recognition mainly because it is experiencing the fastest economic growth rate in the country's history, an average of 6.5 per cent for the last ten years [17]. Without any doubt, therefore, Museveni's government has managed the economy better than any other previous regimes in the Ugandan history.

(iii) Factional Politics

The NRM government has attempted to consolidate national unity, which is the third point on its ten-point programme, through two main policies: (i) by establishing a broad-based national government that seeks to accommodate major interest groups in the country; and (ii) by limiting the activities of political parties, which previously divided the country along both religious and ethnic lines.

While the first policy above has been effective in the sense that former political enemies now sit in the cabinet and govern the country together, the second has been criticized by opposition leaders as being anti-democratic in the sense that it curtails political party competition.

However, it was not until November 1999 that factional politics surfaced in the NRM government, when Col. Kiiza Besigye openly criticized the NRM leadership as being "dishonest", "opportunistic" and "undemocratic". This criticism was embodied in a 14-page statement, which was made available to the media [18].

The significance of this criticism arises from the fact that it came from a strong personality within the National Resistance Movement. Dr. Besigye was among the founding member of the Uganda Patriotic Movement (UPM), a political party led by Yoweri Museveni in contesting the 1980 national elections. In June 1982, Besigye joined Museveni in the bush and was appointed a doctor for the NRA high command, chaired by Museveni himself. When the NRA took over power in 1986, Besigye was appointed Minister of State for Internal Affairs. In 1988, he was appointed the National Political Commissar and Minister of State in the President's office. In 1993, Besigye was appointed the Army Chief of Logistics and

Engineering and promoted to the rank of Colonel. In 1998, he was appointed a Senior Military Advisor to the Minister of State for Defense, a post he still held when he published his criticisms against NRM leadership [19].

Following the publication of Besigye's criticisms, members of the NRM were divided on what should be done. On the one hand, Museveni and his supporters argued in favor of a court martial since, as a Colonel, Besigye could have aired his views through military channels. On the other, supporters of Besigye argued that his criticisms should be debated through NRM channels.

In the end, representatives from Besigye's home district of Rukungiri, in West Uganda, managed to persuade Museveni to pardon Besigye at the same time, however, that the latter was discharged from the army. Shortly after, Besigye declared his intention to stand as a presidential candidate in competition with his former boss, Yoweri Museveni, for the most powerful position in the land. Although Museveni won the presidential election of March 12, 2001, with 69% of the majority vote, fractional politics permeated the campaign process both within and outside the NRM.

(iv) Corruption Within the NRM Government

Defined as a "behavior by public servants, whether elected or appointed, which involves a deviation from his or her formal duties because of reasons of personal gain to himself or herself or to other private persons whom the public servant is associated" [20], corruption has permeated most governments in developing countries. Unfortunately, corruption in Uganda seems to be higher at the moment than ever before. In fact, a report published in October 1999 by Transparency International, a global anti-corruption agency, ranked Uganda in the 11th position among the world's 99 most corrupt countries. On the Corruption Perception Index, which ranges from zero (for most highly corrupt) to ten (for corrupt-free countries), Uganda scored merely 2.2; doing only better than ten of the 99 countries studied [21].

These results seem to be in agreement with two earlier studies, conducted by the World Bank in 1998, on corruption in Uganda. The first was an Integrity Survey funded by the Economic Development Institute of the World Bank. The survey was conducted in 1998 among Ugandan 18,000 households, 1,500 civil servants, and 350 focus groups. The summary of the main findings of this survey were as follows: 40% of household studied reported

231

to have ever paid bribes, especially to members of the police force and the judiciary; majority of the respondents thought that corruption was getting worse; and 70% of respondents thought that there was much corruption in the civil service [22].

The second study was conducted by an anti-corruption mission of the World Bank, that was invited to Uganda by President Musiveni. During the months of September and October 1998, members of this mission met with key government officials, representatives of NGOs, members of the business community, diplomats, members of the press and selected members of the general public. The main conclusions reached after these consultations were: that the prevalence of corruption in Uganda was highest in the areas of procurement and privatisation of public enterprises; and that there was widespread corruption in administration of public revenue and expenditures, political campaigns, public service, and the judiciary [23].

Corruption in Uganda will be discussed along institutional lines. Only three types of institutions will be analysed, partly because they are central within the Ugandan society and partly because corruption in them has been well documented in the media. They are the cabinet, Security institutions and financial institutions. The information utilized in the analysis is mostly from the state-owned newspaper, The New Vision, published daily in Kampala. The period covered is one year, between October 1998 and October 1999.

1. Corruption Within the Cabinet

Between October 1998 and October 1999, two cabinet ministers were forced to resign and three others reshuffled, all on the basis of corruption charges.

On 8th December 1998, a report by the parliamentary select committee on privatisation was presented to the Ugandan Parliament, which especially implicated the minister of state in charge of privatisation (Mr. Matthew Rukikaire) and the state minister of finance for planning and investment (Mr. Sam Kutesa) in financial impropriety and nepotism in the privatisation process. Members of Parliament called for their immediate resignation [24], and in response to that call Rukikaire resigned two days later, on December 10, 1998.

But Kutesa denied using political influence to acquire ground-handling services at Entebbe International Airport, as the report had

233

alleged. His main defence before Parliament was that at the time he acquired shares in the Entebbe Ground Handling Services (ENHAS) he was neither a minister nor a Member of Parliament. The counter argument, however, was simply that when he became a state minister of Finance, under which jurisdiction ENHAS fell, he should at least have resigned his position as chairman of the board of directors of the ENHAS in order to avoid a conflict of interest. The general feeling, both within and outside Parliament, was that ministers should not do business in areas that are under their political influence.

The case against Kutesa, during the debate in the Ugandan Parliament, centred on five main grounds: (i) when he became a minister and chose to continue serving as a chairman of the Board of Directors of the ENHAS, he placed himself in a position of conflict of interest, where he had simultaneously to defend the interest of his company against government interests, contrary to clause 14 (2) of the leadership code of conduct; (ii) on 25 July 1996, Kutesa unilaterally, without the backing of any Board resolution and thereby breaking the law, altered the signatories to all bank accounts of ENHAS, in disfavour of the Uganda Airlines Corporation (UAC) which was then a major shareholder in the company; (iii) being a minister of government and chairman of

ENHAS, Kutesa offered to buy the 50% shares of the UAC at a price below the market value, as determined by an audit firm associated with his private company, thus causing financial loss to government; (iv) during one of the board meetings, Kutesa threatened violence on the UAC representative of the Board, as the latter was defending the interests of a government company against the interests of Kutesa and his company; and (v) as both chairman of ENHAS and minister, Kutesa condoned the financial loss of US$ 445,761 which ENHAS wrote off as a bad debt, thus causing financial loss to the government owned UAC [25].

After a lengthy debate in Parliament, Kutesa's censure motion was supported by 152 votes and opposed by 84 votes. Despite this clear defeat in Parliament, Kutesa refused to resign from the cabinet position till 5th April 1999, when President Museveni dropped his name during a major cabinet reshuffle.

What surprised many Ugandans was the failure of President Museveni to act against corrupt officials in cabinet till his hand was forced by Parliament. A year before Kutesa was censured, Jim Muhwezi (who was then the State Minister of Education) was censured by Parliament after the President had refused to remove him from the cabinet, despite multiple accusations of financial impropriety and political influence peddling levelled against him. Unfortunately, the two ministers that have been censured by Parliament to date happen to be so close to the President ethnically that critics of the current government have interpreted the inaction, on the part of the President, as a reflection of nepotism [26].

The argument by opposition leaders is mainly that the President has always been quick to order for investigation into corruption against government officials who do not share ethnic ties with him. The examples commonly cited by opposition leaders include the former Inspector General of Police (John Odomel) and former Director of Criminal Investigations Department (Chris Bekiza) both of who were suspended, investigated and then dismissed on the order of the President.

Another accusation of corruption within the cabinet, during the period studied, relate to three cabinet ministers in the ministry of agriculture. Dr. Specioza Kazibwe, who was both the Vice President and the Minister of Agriculture, together with her two junior ministers were accused of massive corruption involving the misuse of funds relating to valley dams construction project. About 3.4 billion Ugandan shillings, borrowed from the World Bank, were spent by the ministry in the construction of 15 valley dams, mostly in western Uganda.

Among the accusations levelled against the Vice President and her two junior ministers, by the parliamentary select committee on agriculture after investigating the matter, were: irregularities in the administration of the projects; awarding tenders to fake unregistered construction companies, that ended up doing shoddy work; failure to mobilize people to utilize the constructed dams; and causing financial loss to the government [27].

In response the above accusations, President Musiveni removed Dr. Kazibwe from the Ministry of Agriculture, but retained her as the Vice President. The other two junior ministers were also retained on the cabinet, but reshuffled to other ministries [28].

However, government critics have argued that if these ministers were found wanting in the ministry of agriculture, how could they be good enough for other cabinet responsibilities, especially in relation to the second highest position of the Vice Presidency [29].

2. Corruption within Security Institutions

The discussion on corruption within security institutions is mainly concerned with the military and the police force. The highest level of corruption in the military involved the helicopter scandal. In 1996, the Ugandan military sought to buy four used choppers from the former soviet republic of Belarus. It was alleged that the real price of the four choppers was US$ 6 million although the government was required to pay US$ 12 million, the rest allegedly being kick-backs to the ministry of defense officials. This latter allegation was compounded by the confession of the then defense ministry overseer, Major General Salim Saleh to the President, that he had been offered a commission of US$ 8000,000.00 in the deal relating to the choppers, which he turned down.

The President was subsequently criticized for his failure to constitute an enquiry into the whole deal upon the confession, and that he should have dismissed the Major General, who is also his young brother, for having been involved in a conflict of interest situation where he was both a buyer and seller [30].

Two other factors complicated the choppers deal. First, the only two choppers that were ever delivered to Uganda were not overhauled, as per the contract signed in February 1997, rendering them non-flight-worthy. And second, questions were raised on why the ministry of defence chose to buy the choppers through the company (Consolidated Sales Corporation), which itself bought through other middlemen [31].

Although President Museveni ordered for a probe into allegations surrounding the choppers deal, no conclusive report has been made to the tax- payers.

The failure by the government to investigate this scandal as it unfolded has deepened suspicions, among members of public, that corruption in the military is widespread and left unchecked. Even the President himself has conceded that the main problem in the force is graft by officers who, according to him, sell army property, war materials, food for soldiers and steal money [32]. The President did not mention how the above problems relating to graft in the military were to be addressed.

Corruption in the police force has been so bad that the President forced the Inspector General of Police, John Odomel, to resign in early January 1999 [33], and hardly three months later President Museveni established a Judicial Commission of Inquiry to investigate the Director of the Criminal Investigation Department (CID), Chris Bakiza, and two other senior officers within the CID [34].

The main accusation against Odomel was that his companies were involved in supplying a variety of materials to the police force that he headed, in contravention of police regulations.

As for Bakiza, accusations against him were many and varied, including: allowing his wife to trade with police money [35]; assisting drug dealers for a fee [36]; being involved in livestock fraud worth US$ 4.4 million [37]; being responsible for the death of his girlfriend, who died in his car in 1985 [38]; and receiving bribe to foil investigation of murder cases [39].

Both Odomel and Bakiza were only forced to resign from the police force, with no further punishment for corruption crimes committed. Here, again, an opportunity to effectively deal with corrupt officials, as a deterrence measure to other public officials, was lost.

3. Corruption Within Financial Institutions
Allegations about corruption within financial institutions began after the Privatisation Unit (PU) of the Ministry of Finance sold the

government owned Uganda Commercial Bank (UCB) to a Malaysian Company, Westmont Land Asia, on October 26, 1997. Under the UCB sale agreement, Westmont would not transfer its 49% shares to another party without the authorization of the finance minister. However, in July 1998 The New Vision newspaper came up with a story that Westmont had secretly transferred its shares to a third party without the authority of the Ugandan government.

The controversy generated by this allegation prompted the Ugandan Parliament to set up a special inquiry into the matter, conducted by the select committee on privatisation. But before the committee presented its findings, the Senior Presidential Adviser on Defence, Major General Salim Saleh confessed that he had secretly bought UCB from Westmont using funds from Greenland Investments, where he was both a shareholder and director. Saleh subsequently resigned from his position as a presidential adviser on defence, and the President accepted his resignation [40].

The Bank of Uganda immediately intervened in the management of Greenland Bank by replacing both its Managing Director and the board of directors [41]. And when the Parliament Select Committee on Privatisation presented its report on 9th December 1998, it called, among other things, for the following: immediate

241

cancellation of the UCB-Westmont deal; resignation of all high level officials involved in the privatisation process, including four cabinet ministers; and prosecution for perjury of Major General Salim Saleh and former Managing Director of Greenland bank, Dr. Kiggundu, for having lied to the Parliament Select committee in November 1998 about their involvement in the UCB secret sale deal [42].

The investigation by the Inspector General of Government (IGG) added more detail relating to the controversial sale of the UCB. The 100-page IGG report revealed that under Westmont management, the UCB gave out unsecured loans worth 40 billion Ugandan shillings to companies related to Greenland Investments Limited. The implication of this, according to the IGG report, was that Westmont borrowed money from Greenland to buy UCB, but using UCB itself as a security, and was subsequently paying the money back using cash-flow. The IGG report recommended that the government should recover the money taken out of the UCB, within a period of 45 days, before cancelling the Westmont agreements [43].

The end results of this crisis were mainly five- fold. First, the Ugandan government terminated the contracts by which Westmont had bought 49% shares in the UCB [44]. Second, Greenland sued

Westmont for 23 billion Uganda shilling, which the latter had borrowed to buy 49% shares in the UCB [45]. Third, on April 1, 1999, the Bank of Uganda closed Greenland Bank and its former Managing Director, Dr. Kiggundu, was arrested, charged and remanded in prison for causing the bank a loss of 75 million Ugandan shillings [46]. Fourth, only two of the four cabinet ministers for who Parliament had called for resignation got out of the cabinet; one voluntarily (state minister for privatisation, Matthew Rukikaire) and the other through parliamentary censureship (state minister for investments, Sam Kutesa). Finally, and perhaps most imported of all, Major General Salim Saleh who was at the centre of the crisis was neither tried for perjury, having lied to Parliament, nor punished for his conceded impropriety in the divestiture of the UCB.

Consequences of Corruption in Uganda

To begin with, corruption is always accompanied by financial loss to the government and, by extension, to the taxpayer. For a country like Uganda where more than 66% of the population still live in absolute poverty, as admitted by president Museveni himself [47], heavy losses of funds through corruption undermines the government efforts to reduce poverty in the country.

243

Secondly, corruption in key institutions in Uganda has eroded the confidence that members of the public had for those institutions and the government as a whole. And yet, institutions such as the police force and banks need public support in order to perform effectively.

Third, and closely related to the above point, is the fact that the closure of banks in Uganda as a result of corruption has directly affected depositors' access to their funds. This, in turn, has led to the closure of some businesses, as exemplified by the closure of the Crusader newspaper, which went down with the closure of Greenland bank [48].

Fourth, the investigation of corruption cases, especially by parliamentary committees, has been very expensive for the country. The time and resources spent by MPs in corruption investigations could have been better utilized for more rewarding aspects of national development.

And finally, the privatisation process which previously had been looked upon as a requisite reform for national economic growth has been discredited because of corruption, especially the mishandled sale of the Uganda Commercial Bank.

(v) Museveni's Security Forces

The last criterion on the basis of which the NRM government is compared with previous governments is the nature of security forces. As indicated in chapters four through six, security forces of all previous leaders in Uganda were highly undisciplined and were involved in extra-judicial killings and terrorising the Ugandan society, especially during the leadership of Obote, Amin and Tito Okello.

Fortunately for Uganda, Museveni's National Resistance Army (NRA) that took over power in January 1986 had positive attitudes towards people, which made it popular unlike previous security forces. Although the NRA was later integrated into other armies to constitute the current Uganda People's Defense Force (UPDF), its discipline has made the UPDF superior to all other previous armies in Uganda's history. Moreover, in comparison with his predecessors, Museveni is definitely in control of his armed forces.

However, as discussed in the last section, there has been corruption in the security forces and one of the reasons that president Museveni wanted another term in office was that he wanted to professionalize the army. Museveni's critics have

245

questioned that if he failed to professionalize the army in the previous fifteen years of his uninterrupted rule, how can he do it in the next five years?

Moreover, while state inspired violence that characterized previous regimes had disappeared since the NRM took over power, it seems to have returned in recent years especially through a security organ called Kalangala Action Plan, commanded by Major Kakooza Mutale who is a senior presidential advisor. Particularly during election time, this paramilitary organ has been accused of arresting and intimidating political leaders that are opposed to the movement system.

Finally, high levels of insecurity still punctuate some parts of northern and eastern Uganda where Joseph Kony's Lord Resistance Arm (LRA) rebels have caused havoc, in terms of human lives and property.

NOTES

[1] Museveni, Yoweri, The Path of Liberation, NRM Publications, Kampala, 1989, p.1

[2] Ibid, p. 3

[3] Ibid, p. 5

[4] Ibid, p.7

[5] For this Ten-Point Programme of the NRM, see Yoweri K. Museveni, What is Africa's Problem?, NRM Publications, Kampala, 1992, pp. 279-282. The ten points are: (1) restoration of democracy, (2) restoration of security, (3) consolidation of national unity and elimination of all forms of sectarianism, (4) defending and consolidating national independence, (5) building an independent and integrated self-sustaining national economy, (6) restoration and improvement of social services and rehabilitation of war-ravaged areas, (7) elimination of corruption, (8) redressing errors that have resulted in the dislocation of some sections of the population, (9) co-operation with other African countries, (10) following an economic strategy of a mixed economy.

[6] The Republic of Uganda, The Local Government Act, 1997, Government Printer, Entebbe, 1997

[7] Ibid, section 4.

[8] Ibid, section 46.

[9] Ibid, section 2.

[10] See especially Villaddsen Soren and Francis Lubanga, Democratic Decentralization in Uganda: A New Approach to Local Governance, Fountain Publishers, Kampala, 1996; and Apolo Nsibambi, Decentralization and Civil Service in Uganda: The Quest for Good Governance, Fountain Publishers, Kampala, 1998.

[11] In the presidential elections of 1996, Museveni won with a popular vote of 76%. During the presidential election of March 2001, Museveni won with a popular vote of 69%.

[12] The New Vision, (a Ugandan daily), April 2, 2003.

[13] The Republic of Uganda, Background to the Budget 2000/2001, Ministry of Finance, Planning and Economic Development, Kampala, 2000, p. 53.

[14] The New Vision , December 21, 2000.
[15] The New Vision, December 18, 2000.

[16] The Republic of Uganda, <u>The Budget Speech 2000/2001</u>, Ministry of Finance, Planning and Economic Development, Kampala, p. 9.

[17] The Republic of Uganda, <u>Background to the Budget 2000/2001</u>, pp. 9-11.

[18] <u>Sunday Vision</u>, November 7, 1999.

[19] <u>The New Vision</u>, March 17, 2001.

[20] Lapalombora, Joseph, "Structural and Institutional Aspects of Corruption", <u>Social Research</u>, Vol. 61, 1994, p. 328.

[21] <u>The New Vision</u>, October 28, 1999.

[22] <u>The New Vision,</u> December 10, 1998.

[23] <u>The New Vision</u>, December 10, 1998.

[24] <u>The New Vision</u>, December 10, 1998.
[25] <u>The New Vision</u>, March 3, 1999.

[26] This interpretation has been reinforced by the fact that both Jim Muhwezi and Sam Kutesa have been re-appointed as cabinet ministers by Museveni, following the latter's presidential victory in 2001.

[27] The New Vision, January 13, 1999.

[28] The New Vision, April 16, 1999.

[29] The Monitor (another Ugandan daily), April 12, 1999.

[30] The Monitor, October 29, 1998.

[31] The New Vision, January 10, 1999.

[32] The New Vision, February 7, 1999.
[33] The New Vision, January 3, 1999.

[34] The New Vision, March 25, 1999.

[35] The New Vision, May 27, 1999.
[36] The New Vision, May 28, 1999.

[37] The New Vision, June 18, 1999.

[38] The New Vision, August 20, 1999.

[39] The New Vision, August 30, 1999.

[40] The New Vision, December 7, 1998.

[41] The Monitor, December 7, 1998.

[42] The New Vision, December 8, 1998.

[43] The New Vision, February 9, 1999.

[44] The New Vision, March 11, 1999.

[45] The New Vision, March 25, 1999.

[46] The New Vision, April 2, 1999.

[47] The New Vision, October 10, 1998.
[48] The New Vision, April 3, 1999.

CHAPTER VIII

SUMMARY AND RECOMMENDATIONS ARISING OUT OF THE STUDY

(1) Summary

The early chapters in this study sought to demonstrate the extent to which the politicization of cultural cleavages in Uganda during the colonial period laid a foundation for future economic and political conflicts among sub-national groups in the country.

As the analysis in chapter two indicated, the uneven colonial penetration that entailed differential access to modern education, economy, and socio-political structures led to uneven development among sub-national groups in Uganda. This, in turn, provoked and intensified competition and conflict between the privileged and the underprivileged sub-national groups at the national, regional and local levels.

Further constraints on political order in Uganda arose from the development of colonial political structures, which were intended to transform Uganda's traditional society. As indicated in chapter three, the colonial administration made efforts to ensure that boundaries separating the basic local administrative units (districts) corresponded with lines of ethnic divisions, on the grounds that the enforcement of law and order would be easier and less expensive under this arrangement. However, power inequalities developed among these territorially as well as culturally based institutions mainly because of the differential treatment that they received from the colonial government, with the result that competition and conflict developed among them.

Such competition and conflict were exacerbated by the Independence Constitution, which gave legal recognition to power inequalities that had earlier developed among these districts. For, as indicated in chapter four, this Constitution stratified Uganda into three unequal parts. At the apex was Buganda that was granted full federal status, on the basis of which its historical privileged status within Uganda was recognized and preserved. Below Buganda were the kingdoms of western Uganda each of which was granted semi-federal status, intended to preserve its monarchical institutions. At the bottom of this power hierarchy were non-kingdom districts whose relationship with the central government was made unitary, implying that the latter was to control them more closely than had been the case hitherto.

This ambiguous colonial legacy, together with Obote's unsteady style of leadership, constituted the main sources of political disorder during the early years of post-colonial Uganda. Problems attaining national significance soon after Uganda's independence included: a conflict over territory which Bunyoro had lost to Buganda at the establishment of colonial rule in Uganda; Buganda's relationship to the centre; and a struggle for power between the political elites from the federal-oriented southern Uganda, on the one hand, and those from the unitary-oriented northern Uganda on the other. As indicated in chapter five, the attempted solutions to some of these problems led to further political disorder in the country.

The return of lost territory to Bunyoro, as decided through a referendum that was held in the disputed area in 1964, provoked strong resentment among the Baganda. And with the support of political elites from southern Uganda as well as from Shaban Opolot -- the then commander of the Uganda Army -- the Baganda sought to remove Obote from the leadership of the country. As a countermove against this threat, most political elites from northern Uganda, including Idi Amin -- the then Deputy Commander of the Uganda Army -- rallied behind Obote. During this struggle for power, which led to the constitutional crisis of 1966, the Obote coalition utilized the northern-dominated Ugandan security forces to subdue its southern political opponents.

Moreover, with the help of these forces, Obote detained five key ministers from southern Uganda; abrogated the Independence Constitution and replaced it with an interim one, which abolished all elements of federalism and all the privileges associated with them; dismissed the Army Commander and subsequently replaced him with Idi Amin; deposed President Edward Mutesa and assumed the powers of an executive president; ordered government troops to take over Mutesa's palace, leading to the latter's flight into exile in England where he later died; and established a unitary republic in which all districts in the country were subordinated to the direct control of the central government.

In so doing, Obote overcame some sources of political disorder that had been inherited from the colonial period, including Bunyoro's lost territory, Buganda's privileged status, and power inequalities that had existed among local governments. However, these Obote achievements were realized at the cost of his becoming a personal ruler par excellence.

As indicated in chapter five, personal rule entails, among other things, the leader's excessive reliance on personal loyalty both within and outside the security forces; and the leader's use of coercion to enforce public compliance. During and after the 1966 constitutional crisis in Uganda, Obote's leadership was essentially based on these elements.

With the legitimacy of his leadership increasingly in decline, Obote established a personal security force -- the General Service Unit (GSU) -- which, together with the regular Uganda Army, constituted the power base for his regime during the late 1960s. However, struggles for power and control began to develop, first between the regular army and the GSU, and second, between President Obote and General Amin who was then the Army Commander. As indicated in the later part of chapter five, these conflicts culminated in Amin's military coup of January 1971, which removed Obote from power.

Amin's coming to power in 1971 marked a transition from personal to dictatorial rule in Uganda, which entailed less institutional control and more coercion. In theory, a dictator exercises his power through absolute control of the traditional means of coercion, which include the army, police, bureaucracy, and judiciary [1].

As indicated in chapter six, Amin not only controlled such means of coercion, but like Obote before him, he developed his own personal security forces -- the misnamed State Research Bureau and the Public Safety Unit -- which he utilized to penetrate and terrorize Uganda society. All these repressive controls over the state and society by Amin culminated in both political and economic decay in the country, as indicated in the later part of chapter six.

Given Amin's legacy and the inability of post-Amin regimes to establish political order, political violence and instability in Uganda continued, leading to rapid changes of leadership and eventually to a return to military rule. As indicated in chapter seven, all post-Amin regimes failed either to acquire popular legitimacy or to restore order and/or internal security. Instead, they were characterized by high levels of internal sectionalism, widespread corruption, and of indiscipline within their security forces. The main challenge to Museveni's current regime, therefore, has been to overcome these sources of political disorder that had previously plagued the Ugandan system.

As indicated in chapter seven, the NRM government has been successful in dealing with some sources of political disorder at the same time that it has failed to deal with others. On the positive side, the NRM government has rehabilitated the economy through the following actions: the 1987 currency reform that brought down inflation; rehabilitation of roads; reduction in smuggling; returning of expropriated property to Asians, thereby encouraging foreign investment; and raising levels of tax collection 22.7 times over (from 44 billion Ugandan shillings in 1988 to 1000 billion shillings in the year 2000).

The impact of the above actions has been far reaching. First, the amount of poverty in Uganda has fallen by 21% under NRM leadership [2]. Second, as a result of universal primary education, primary school enrolment has more than doubled. And finally, according to IMF and World Bank statistics, the annual growth rate of the Ugandan economy in the 1990s was more than 7% [3]; a performance that has stimulated more international aid, including debt relief.

Apart from the economy, the NRM leadership has attained a higher level of legitimacy than any of the previous regimes as reflected, among other things, by successfully calling two consecutive national elections, both presidential and parliamentary. Secondly, the broad-based government that characterized the initial NRM regime was more integrative than otherwise. Third, extra-judicial killings by security forces have been curtailed, and the army has been under control unlike the previous ones. And finally, both human rights and freedom of the press have greatly improved.

On the negative side, some critics argue that corruption and nepotism have never been worse [4]. Unfortunately, many Ugandans, especially from rural areas, feel that they have not enjoyed the benefits of the growing economy because of rampant corruption in high circles of government. Second, the rebel activities especially in northern Uganda has partly undermined the credibility of the regime as reflected, among other things, in low vote for Museveni from northern Uganda during the March 2001 presidential elections. Thirdly, Uganda's involvement in the war in the Congo had three negative impacts: it was expensive, it took much of the president's valuable time, and it damaged president Museveni's reputation both at home and abroad [5]. Finally, the movement system has not been as inclusive and non-partisan as it claims, as reflected in the manner in which the NRM leadership treats any opposition, whether real or imagined. Critics look at the

NRM system as a one party state intended to maintain and enrich those in power [6].

On balance, however, the record of the NRM government still remains superior to those of all its predecessors. President Museveni has been a result-oriented performer and has accomplished a lot for Uganda. But it is unclear why he has been unable to fight corruption head on, and save his leadership from that tainted image.

(2) Policy Recommendations.

On the basis of both theory and history, the ability of a developing country to attain political order seems to depend largely on the ability of its leaders to acquire power and legitimacy to rule effectively. Therefore, the recommendations that will be made below address primarily those areas whose improvement is likely to lead to the attainment of effective, authoritative, and legitimate government. At least four of such areas are particularly vital for Uganda: social and economic disparities, imbalances in the distribution of political power, violation of human rights, and the persistence of corruption within nerves of government.

(i) **Reduction of Social and Economic Disparities**: While social and economic disparities exist in all countries, developed as well as underdeveloped, they tend to be more salient in the latter for two main reasons. First, most of those who control the state apparatus in underdeveloped countries not only have expanded their wealth and privilege through both corruption and benefits accruing from dependent development, they have also been central in creating, reinforcing, and maintaining inequalities. And second, regional disparities in most post-colonial states like Uganda tend to promote ethnic competition and conflict, mainly because of the previous uneven colonial penetration. Under such circumstances, intense social conflicts have been a common feature in most developing countries, including Uganda.

Hence, government efforts to encourage balanced social and economic development at the national, regional, and local levels would be particularly vital in promoting political order in Uganda. Such government efforts would include policies aimed at: (i) bridging socio-economic gaps between the urban rich and the rural poor, and (ii) narrowing inequalities between the more developed southern and the underdeveloped northern parts of Uganda. The first policy calls for a dynamic rural development strategy, based on essential human needs and a long-term plan directed towards income redistribution. The second calls for sacrificing some national growth for the sake of regional socio-economic parity, without which competition and conflict, mostly aggravated by ethnic overtones, are likely to continue to rise.

(ii) Balancing Political Power: In a multi-ethnic state like Uganda, where cultural cleavages have long been politicized, rule by any single ethnic group is likely to result in other ethnic groups' being insecure and alienated. Both Obote and Amin largely fashioned their personal security forces from their respective ethnic groups. The result in both cases was the tyranny of the wider Ugandan society by the ethnic group in power. To avoid repetition of such leaderships, which in the past have led to high levels of political violence and instability, it should be a government policy to establish political procedures that allow for the accommodation of all major segments of Ugandan society at all important levels of the decision-making process.

Inherent in such a policy, commonly known as consociationalism [7], are two vital principles: proportional representation and grand coalition government. While the former requires that government bureaucracies, including security forces, should be representative

263

of the larger society, in both outlook and composition, the latter requires that political leaders of all major segments in the country should share power and be willing to accommodate each others' views in their quest for political order and stability in the country as a whole. As David Apter correctly observed in reference to Uganda, "behind the question of parliamentary forms and constitutional arrangements lies the need to create a genuine basis of association of all groups, whether ethnic, racial, or class" [8].

In my view, Apter's recommendation is even more valid now than it was on the eve of Uganda's political independence when he made it, for, in the absence of such genuine association among sub-national groups in Uganda, more recurrent patterns of political disorder and other forms of political decay have since developed and become institutionalized [9].

(iii) Respect for Human Rights: At least two conditions seem to be closely associated with violation of human rights in developing countries: (i) lack of legitimacy on the part of both political institutions and the leadership; and (ii) a general absence of internal security in the country. With these conditions in place, arbitrary use of instruments of coercion by the leadership (state violence) has become a common practice in developing countries.

Under such circumstances, the attainment of political order largely depends on the establishment of a legitimate government whose leaders have a high respect for both institutional procedures and human dignity.

(iv) Rehabilitation of the Economy: Economic dislocations in Uganda have arisen from three main sources: (i) the structural dependence of the economy; (ii) the general lack of national economic policies which are internally consistent and/or coherent; and (iii) the persistence of corruption.

The reduction of Uganda's external economic dependence requires at least two related policies. First, there should be a persistent government policy to diversify the country's export commodities rather than depending on coffee and cotton. Given the fertile land with which Uganda is endowed, that country could easily become the food basket of its neighboring countries. And second, Uganda could also reduce its import trade dependence by establishing a consistent government policy that emphasizes internally oriented development planning based primarily on domestic needs. Hence, horticulture industry should be particularly encouraged and supported in Uganda.

265

The success of the above recommendations, however, largely depends on the extent to which national economic policies remain consistent over time. In the past, each of the various regimes that ruled Uganda has advocated its own national economic policies. However, since any viable national economy requires long-term economic planning, it would be highly desirable that the formulation of national economic policies be entrusted to civil service economic experts, whose decisions and advice should be respected by political leaders, even when governments change.

(v) Handling Corruption: Uganda does not have sufficient trained manpower, especially in the judiciary, to enforce anti-corrupt laws effectively and judiciously. In fact, President Museveni blames the judiciary for the persistence of corruption in Uganda. According to him, the means of investigation, prosecution and judgment of cases relating to corruption is lacking. He has even suggested that he was considering hiring judges from abroad to hasten resolution of corruption cases [10].

The first recommendation relating to corruption, therefore, is that institutions for enforcing anti-corruption laws need to be made stronger than they are now. In particular, the office of the Inspector General of Government (IGG) needs to be expanded and to be given more resources and power than it has at the moment. As well, the judiciary should be given more resources to enable it do its work more effectively. For, in the final analysis, if corruption was curtailed by effective institutions the government would most likely save more money than it would have paid to make those institutions stronger.

The second recommendation relates to the failure by President Museveni to live to his own words in relation to punishing corrupt officials. On 11th December 1998, Museveni told the press that he was "ready to put anybody behind bars and confiscate legally their properties if they got them the wrong way". The President emphasized the point that "anybody who causes financial loss to the government will pay back that money" [11]. Yet, the worst that has happened to Museveni's corrupt cabinet ministers was firing them, with no compensation to the government for financial losses they caused. Where benefits derived from corruption are high and the risk of punishment is very low, corruption is bound to be rampant. The recommendation arising from this is that proven corrupt official not only should be imprisoned, but should also refund all the money embezzled and lose any property acquired fraudulently.

267

The mismanagement of the privatisation of state enterprises in Uganda has created fertile grounds for corruption. More often than not, the privatisation process in Uganda has hardly been transparent, making it easy for a practice of kick-backs to develop between public officials, who manage the process, and their clients. Hence, the final recommendation relates to the privatisation process in Uganda. Not only should the entire process become transparent, but also public officials who run it should be forced to pay for financial losses when they do occur. In other words transparency and accountability should be the guiding principles for the privatisation process in Uganda.

NOTES

[1] See Franz Neumann, <u>The Democratic and the Authoritarian State,</u> New York, Free Press, 1957, pp.214-224.

[2] Anna Borzello, "Poll Challenger Rattles Ugandan President", <u>Guardian Unlimited</u>, March 9, 2001.

[3] Ali Mutassa, "Uganda's Election Issues", <u>BBC News World Service</u>, March 1, 2001.

[4] Ibid

[5] Feeling the Pulse with Canrad Nkutu, <u>New Vision</u>, November 1, 1998.

[6] Simon Tisdall, "A Good Man in Africa?", <u>Guardian Unlimited</u>, March 15, 2001

[7] For a review and discussion of the theory of consociationalism, see Arend Lijphart, <u>Democracy in Plural Societies: A Comparative Exploration</u>, New Have Yale University Press, 1977.

[8] David Apter, <u>The Political Kingdom in Uganda: A Study of Bureaucratic Nationalism</u>, Princeton, Princeton University Press, 1961, p. 477.

[9] It was alleged, for example, that one of the presidential aspirant from Eastern Uganda, during the 2001 presidential elections in Uganda, said that: " it was time for easterners to eat". See <u>The New Vision</u>, December 18, 2000.

[10] <u>The New Vision</u>, December 10, 1998.

[11] <u>The New Vision</u>, December 12, 1998.

www.ingramcontent.com/pod-product-compliance
Lightning Source LLC
Chambersburg PA
CBHW020606270326
41927CB00005B/202